Mexican Americans
and the Politics of Diversity

THE MEXICAN AMERICAN EXPERIENCE

Adela de la Torre, EDITOR

Mexican Americans
and the Politics of Diversity

¡Querer es poder!

Lisa Magaña

The University of Arizona Press   Tucson

The University of Arizona Press
© 2005 The Arizona Board of Regents
All rights reserved

10   09   08   07   06   05   6   5   4   3   2   1

Library of Congress Cataloging-in-Publication Data

Magaña, Lisa.
   Mexican Americans and the politics of diversity : querer es
poder! / Lisa Magaña.
      p. cm. — (The Mexican American experience)
   Includes bibliographical references and index.
   ISBN 13: 978-0-8165-2265-1 (pbk. : alk. paper)
   ISBN 10: 0-8165-2265-0 (pbk. : alk. paper)
   1. Mexican Americans—Politics and government. 2. Political
participation—United States. I. Title. II. Series.
E184.M5M353 2005
324'.0896872073—dc22
                              2005004940

This book is dedicated to Robert, Isabella, and Sofia.

■ CONTENTS

◼ LIST OF ILLUSTRATIONS

FIGURES

TABLES

■ ACRONYMS USED IN THE TEXT

AWOC	Agricultural Workers Organizing Committee
CAWP	Center for American Women and Politics
INS	Immigration and Naturalization Service
LRU	La Raza Unida Party
LULAC	League of United Latin American Citizens
MALDEF	Mexican American Legal Defense and Educational Fund
MEChA	Movimiento Estudiantil Chicano de Aztlán
MELA	Mothers of East Los Angeles
NALEO	National Association of Latino Elected and Appointed Officials
NCLR	National Council of La Raza
UFW	United Farm Workers of America
VRA	Voting Rights Act

◼ ACKNOWLEDGMENTS

The contributions of several people made this book possible. I would first like to acknowledge my research assistants, James Garcia, Lizette Morales, and Arturo Valdivia, for their help in gathering, writing, and synthesizing information. I am also grateful to colleagues and staff in the Chicana/o Studies Department at Arizona State University, particularly Alma Alvarez, Cordelia Candelaria, Edward Escobar, and Vera Galaviz for their assistance in completing this project. As always, my family and friends have provided support and encouragement to complete this book and I am grateful. Finally, I would like thank Patti Hartmann, my editor, for her guidance, patience, and support throughout this book.

■ INTRODUCTION

As a Mexican American political scientist who studies political participation and public policy formation, I am often asked why my community does not care about politics. This is a popular misconception that has powerful implications. A group that is perceived to be politically apathetic is more likely to be ignored, taken for granted, and even scapegoated or blamed for problems. I remind people that political participation is not defined solely by **voter turnout** or being a member of a political party. If political participation is assessed from a variety of viewpoints and in a multitude of settings, it is clear that Mexican Americans are, in fact, very politically active and do care about politics.

This book is an examination of the various ways politics plays out in the Mexican-origin community, including voter turnout, elected representation, **grassroots** strategies, public policy creation, and the influence of **lobbying** organizations, to name but a few. The significance of analyzing various approaches to political participation, rather than just electoral turnout, is demonstrated by the fact that immigrants, who are not able to vote because they are not U.S. citizens, make up as much as 40 percent of the Mexican-origin population nationwide. In some communities, this figure is even higher. Yet, noncitizens of Mexican origin can influence U.S. public policy through a variety of political activities. For instance, Mexican-origin noncitizens marched in opposition to **Proposition 187,** bringing national attention to this voter-approved initiative that would have virtually banned publicly funded services for immigrants in California in 1994. (The initiative passed but was overturned in the courts.)

Mexican Americans are a relatively young ethnic group. School dropout and poverty rates are higher among Mexican Americans than other major ethnic groups in the United States. Citizenship rates among Mexican American communities are often lower than those in the general population. These **demographic** characteristics do account for lower levels of voter participation than is true of other groups such as Anglos or African Americans. Yet, the lower level of direct electoral participation does not mean that Mexican Americans are apolitical. On the contrary, this book illustrates the essential roles Mexican Americans play in organizing strategies, community involvement, policy debates, and lobby- and interest-group participation. In the last decade, there has been significant political

mobilization around issues such as environmental racism, immigration, and **affirmative action.**

Given that Mexican Americans are the fastest growing minority ethnic group, surpassing African Americans, the nation's major political parties are targeting Mexican American voters like never before. For the first time during the 2000 presidential campaign, the Republican and Democratic Parties ran commercials on Spanish-language television networks. In states across the nation, the Mexican American vote can now mean the difference between winning or losing an election.

After reading this book, you will have a better understanding of Mexican American political participation at the local, state, and federal levels. You will be able to identify the historical, socioeconomic, and theoretical factors that result in political participation. You will learn about successful political mobilization strategies in the Mexican American community while considering the future implications of Mexican American participation in politics. Most important, after reading this book, you will understand that Mexican American political participation and the community's public policy needs are often unique. A theme that runs throughout this book is that Mexican Americans are a diverse political group whose interests and needs cannot be easily pigeonholed. But given the demographic trends and projections for ongoing growth of this population, Mexican Americans will continue to participate in both electoral and non-electoral political outlets.

To illustrate real-life issues relevant to Mexican American politics, I have relied on books, journal articles, policy reports, surveys and government evaluations, and newspaper articles. I have also interviewed Mexican Americans, who give insights into the everyday political needs of the group. These interviewees were all of Mexican origin but represent various age groups and a variety of professional and personal interests.

▪ Interviewee Personal Profiles

JOSE M. L. ARAGON is a twenty-one-year-old college student born in Northridge, California. He is majoring in political science.

ANA YELI CONTRERAS is nineteen years old and was born in Guanajuato, Mexico. She is a student majoring in bilingual elementary education (see figure 1).

■ I. Ana Yeli Contreras

EDUARDO DELCI is a sixty-three-year-old counselor and community activist (see figure 2). He was born in Mesa, Arizona.

JENNIFER DRURY is a twenty-two-year-old math and English tutor. She was born in Brawley, California.

VERA GALAVIZ is a fifty-six-year-old office manager who was born in Phoenix, Arizona (see figure 3).

R. JOYCE ZAMORA LAUSCH, a thirty-one-year-old professor of literature, was born in Boulder, Colorado.

JOHN LEAÑOS is a thirty-four-year-old artist born in Pomona, California.

JOAQUIN LOPEZ, a twenty-three-year-old intervention specialist, was born in San Diego, California.

CHRISTINE MARIN is a librarian and archivist born in Globe, Arizona.

FRANCES MARQUEZ is a thirty-six-year-old political organizer and scholar born in Montebello, California.

2. Eduardo Delci

MATHEW MARTINEZ is thirty years old. Born in Española, New Mexico, he is currently an instructor at Macalester College while completing his doctorate in American studies there.

MIGUEL MONTIEL is a sixty-one-year-old professor of **Chicano** studies. He was born in Nogales, Arizona.

■ 3. Vera Galaviz

GRACE NAGY is a forty-six-year-old technical specialist born in Los Angeles, California.

VIRGINIA PESQUIERA is a sixty-two-year-old educator born in Tucson, Arizona (see figure 4).

PAUL QUESADA is a twenty-seven-year-old police officer born in Silver City, New Mexico.

■ Organization of the Book

Mexican Americans and the Politics of Diversity is intended to be accessible to a variety of readers, particularly those who are examining Mexican American politics for the first time. To this end, each chapter provides discussion questions as well as references for further research on the topic. The text is presented in six chapters. Chapter 1 examines the demographic characteristics of Mexican Americans and how these factors influence their political participation. Research on Mexican American political participation is relatively new. I review briefly some of the important research regarding Mexican American politics. Specifically, age, family structure, education level, income, residence, and place of birth have much influence

■ 4. Virginia Pesquiera

on this population's participation in both **traditional politics** and **nontraditional politics**.

Chapter 2 explores Mexican Americans (and other **Latino** groups) in a historical context by illustrating the major events that led to the community's political participation and activism today. Mexican Americans have confronted discrimination and prejudice throughout their history in the United States. With regard to voting patterns, physical and psychological barriers, such as forced segregation, discriminatory literacy tests, and poll taxes, were imposed to discourage voter participation. Congress approved the **Voting Rights Act** (VRA) of 1965 to eliminate many of these barriers and encourage greater minority participation in the political process. Civil rights lawsuits by Mexican American and other Latino organizations became important agents of change at all levels of politics. Among these organizations were the National Association of Latino Elected and Appointed Officials (NALEO), the National Council of La Raza (NCLR), the League of United Latin American Citizens (LULAC), and the Mexican American Legal Defense and Educational Fund (MALDEF), to name but a few. Mainstream political organizations are also responding to the large and growing Mexican community that resides in the United States. Organizations that are **binational** in focus are also gaining more political importance.

Chapter 3 examines Mexican American participation in electoral political outlets, including party affiliation, voter turnout, and attitudes toward policy issues as well as political parties. Today, about two-thirds of Mexican American voters are Democrats, largely due to familiarity with the party, the region where these voters reside, outreach by the party, and ideological preferences. A more recent trend reflects a small but growing shift in the community toward joining the Republican Party as well as lesser-known political parties, or registering as Independents.

In Chapter 4, I examine a variety of reasons for increasing political participation by Mexican American women. Among these are unprecedented outreach by political parties and elected officials, as well as growth in political participation by women generally. It is important to note that women, regardless of their **ethnicity** or socioeconomic status, tend to be more involved than men in politics at the local level and for personal reasons. This means that Mexican American women are, in fact, politically active, even though their involvement may not take conventional forms.

Chapter 5 explores the issues and public policies that are most important to Mexican Americans. Education, community issues, housing, health care, and employment are just some of the topics explored in this chapter. These issues are among the most significant ones shaping Mexican American political participation.

The final chapter presents general recommendations and predictions regarding Mexican American political participation based on the demographic, cultural, and historical determinants of this population. Undoubtedly, Mexican Americans are an important political force and will continue to be in the coming decades. This chapter looks at how political issues will affect this growing and dynamic population.

Throughout this book I use the term *Mexican American* to refer to U.S. citizens who are of Mexican ancestry. When I wish to encompass Mexican Americans and those born in Mexico who are living in the United States, I use *Mexican origin*. *Immigrant* refers to non–U.S. citizens who are residing in the United States, whether legally or illegally. *Chicana/o* also refers to individuals who are of Mexican origin, particularly those who were activists during the 1960s and 1970s Chicano Movement. *Latino* refers to U.S. residents who are of Mexican, Cuban, Puerto Rican, or Central American origin.

Mexican Americans
and the Politics of Diversity

Conceptualizing Mexican American Politics

Prior to the 1960s, research on Mexican American political participation was scant. This was attributable partly to the low numbers of Mexican Americans participating in electoral politics generally, and partly to scholars ignoring their political importance. Within the last forty years, however, studies on the group have flourished.

Conceptualizing or describing Mexican Americans as a population is not simple. Even though their presence is large and growing, Mexican Americans are considered a minority group because they confront differential and unequal treatment (Blea 1992). They are also considered an ethnic group because they are characterized by distinct cultural practices, religion, and language (Takaki 1994). Not all Mexican Americans are Spanish speaking, however, and not all have immigrant influences. Some Mexican Americans are newly arrived immigrants whereas others have family histories in the United States that go back hundreds of years. Scholars would also describe Mexican Americans as a colonized group, a culture that has been dominated by a larger more aggressive power for generations, and as a result has lost aspects of its unique **identity** (Barrera 1979). Furthermore, the Mexican American community is also socioeconomically diverse: Some are poor whereas others are experiencing economic prosperity. Given all the diversity within the group, it is no surprise that understanding or describing its political activities is difficult at best.

As evidence, some Mexican Americans see identifying themselves with one group label, such as defining themselves as Chicana/o or Latina/o, as an impediment to political empowerment. A label can be a source of pride for a group. On the other hand, inaccurate, demeaning, or inflammatory labels may weaken social movements and overgeneralize the needs of the group. In short, it would be inaccurate and disingenuous to assert that Mexican Americans have a distinct political identity. Cutting-edge scholars continue to examine and redefine the best way to portray them in order to understand their political behavior (Bedolla 2000).

How Mexican Americans will vote on certain issues is a major area for exploration (García and de la Garza 1985). How long a person has lived in the United States has much to do with how he or she views political and policy issues relating to immigration, education, and the environment (DeSipio 1996). Even language preference influences an individual's political identity (de la Garza et al. 1992). The socio-**demographic** characteristics of Mexican Americans that limit their political electoral participation, including youth, economic status, and the proportion of foreign born individuals in the overall population, are also evaluated in the research.

Another method of interpretation focuses on level of representation; that is, how many Mexican Americans are holding political office relative to the total population (Fraga, Meier, and England 1986). Scholars also examine the level of political outreach targeting Mexican American voters, noting that targeting Mexican Americans makes them more likely to participate in electoral politics (Grofman 1992). A relatively new area of political research relates to Mexican American women as elected leaders and political players (Marquez 2003) as well as the characteristics of Mexican American female elected officials (Montoya et al. 2000; Takash 1993).

Grassroots political participation research focuses on organizing movements at the local level. These actions are characterized by groups that demand action on a particular problem or issue, such as civil rights reform, racial equality, environmental racism, or gender equity, to name but a few (Torres and Katsiaficas 1999). These movements do not activate the society at large, as in more **traditional politics.** Grassroots movements are difficult to maintain for extended periods. Research on grassroots movements illustrates significant political fervor in the Mexican American community, even though these actions may be overlooked by traditional political science research (Pardo 1998; Pulido 1996).

Political organizations are another essential area of study for understanding Mexican American politics. Typically there are three types of Mexican American organizations: (1) mutualistas, social groups formed to assist newly arrived Mexican immigrants with adjusting to their new homes; (2) unions, organizations formed to deal with employment and community empowerment issues; and (3) contemporary organizations, essentially **lobbying** and interest groups that take on distinct agendas (Marquez 2003). These types of organizations are powerful allies for the Mexican American community and illustrate the evolving political agendas of the community.

Trying to assess political attitudes is another area of research. Do Mexican Americans in general define themselves as politically **conservative, liberal,** or moderate? For instance, politically conservative values held by many Mexican Americans include opposing abortion and espousing the values of Catholicism, issues that traditionally appeal to social conservatives. Yet Mexican Americans also advocate many traditionally liberal notions, such as support for big government, more lenient immigration regulation, and more government-provided services for individuals who need assistance (Suro 1998). Studies, such as surveys assessing political attitudes, indicate that Mexican Americans are not easily categorized and can be defined as both liberal and conservative.

Another area debated by scholars is whether Mexican Americans are politically assimilated. Assimilation refers to the process of taking on the norms and practices of the culture at large, and it is directly influenced by the number of immigrants that make up a population. In the past, the study of immigrants and the process of assimilation often focused on European immigrants who came to the country at the turn of the century, such as the Irish or Germans. Their migration patterns were measurable, and almost all these individuals stayed in the United States permanently, in part because of the difficulty and cost of traveling back to their homelands. With subsequent generations, these groups became assimilated and defined themselves as Americans. For Mexicans, immigration is constant, and immigrants can move back and forth between Mexico and the United States several times. Many Mexican Americans, particularly in the first and second generations, also maintain strong ties to family and hometowns in Mexico. The influences from both Mexico and the United States are strong and result in what some scholars define as an acculturated culture, one that retains two identities. The process of forgoing one's culture of origin for U.S. mainstream culture does not occur nearly as frequently or rapidly for Mexican Americans as for previous immigrant groups, and scholars want to know how this process influences their political participation.

■ Mexican Americans: A Demographic Profile

It is also important to consider the demographic characteristics of the Mexican-origin population—such as income, age, and citizenship status—in order to explain their political participation. In general, the Mexican American population has escalated in the last thirty years. Demographic

Table 1 Total U.S. population and U.S. Latino population, 1950–2004

DATE	U.S. POPULATION (in millions)	U.S. LATINO POPULATION	PERCENTAGE LATINO
1950	151.3	4.0	2.6
1960	179.3	6.9	3.8
1970	203.2	9.0	4.4
1980	226.5	14.6	6.4
1989	249.4	23.7	9.5
1994	259.3	25.5	9.9
1996	264.8	27.2	10.3
1998	268.8	30.5	11.3
2000	281.4	35.3	12.5
2002	288.2	38.6	13.4
2004	296.1	43.5	14.7

Source: U.S. Census Bureau 2000b.

Table 2 Countries of origin of U.S. Latino population, 2004

NATIONALITY	POPULATION (in millions)	PERCENTAGE OF HISPANIC POPULATION
Mexican	28.948	66.5
Central American	3.954	9.1
Puerto Rican	3.831	8.8
South American	2.300	5.3
Cuban	1.675	3.8
Dominican	1.305	3.0
Other	1.517	3.5
Total	43.530	100

Source: Therrien and Ramirez 2000.

predictions of continued growth make the Mexican American population an attractive political powerhouse.

First consider the overall growth of the **Latino** population. In the 1950s, there were only four million Latinos (2.6 percent) in the total U.S. population; today there are more than forty-three million, making up 14.7 percent

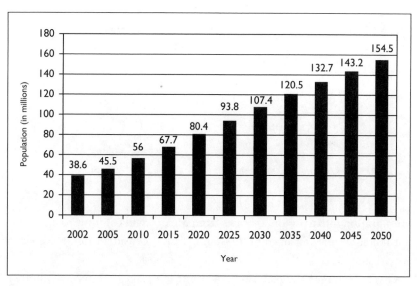

■ 5. U.S. Latino population projections, in millions (Source: 2004 U.S. Hispanic Market Report, Synovate, Inc.)

of the total U.S. population (see table 1). Of the total Latino population, people of Mexican origin make up 66 percent (see table 2). Puerto Ricans account for 9 percent, Cubans for 4 percent, and Central and South Americans combined for 14.7 percent (Therrien and Ramirez 2000).

Projections indicate that Latinos will continue to be an important force in politics in the years to come. As of 2002, the Census Bureau estimates that Latinos became the largest minority group in the United States (excluding Puerto Rico), surpassing African Americans. By 2020, the overall Latino population is projected to be approximately eighty million—meaning one in every five U.S. residents will be of Latino origin, and by 2050, the population will be approximately 156 million—or one of every four U.S. residents (U.S. Census Bureau 2004; see figure 5).

Mexico is the largest Latin American country, with 100.4 million people. Needless to say, its close proximity to the United States, and the dramatic difference in standard of living between the neighboring countries, makes the latter the preferred destination for Mexican immigrants. Consequently, the United States has become the fifth largest Latino country in the world. Nearly 50 percent of the current Mexican-origin population in the United States is foreign born, meaning that immigration accounts for a large percentage of the population growth. Demographers predict that

Table 3 Mexican American population percentages by U.S. region

U.S. REGION	PERCENTAGE
South	35.0
Midwest	23.2
West	22.8
Northeast	19.0
Total	100.0

Source: U.S. Census Bureau 2000b, table 1.1.

immigration into the United States from Mexico will continue to be high if not increase, making immigration an essential consideration in Mexican American politics.

Given the large foreign-born population, language preference is another important demographic characteristic. Researchers estimate that 70 percent of **Hispanics** speak some Spanish, with 40 percent describing themselves as using no English at all. This demographic characteristic means that Spanish-language media outlets must be used to approach this group. Almost half of this population must receive its information from Spanish-language television networks and newspapers, or they simply will not be informed on pressing political issues. Moreover, rates of citizenship among the foreign born are relatively low, leaving large numbers of Mexican Americans disenfranchised.

Another important consideration is where the Mexican-origin population resides. Approximately 50 percent of the overall Hispanic population lives in central cities rather than rural areas. Furthermore, the majority of Mexicans and Mexican Americans live in the U.S. Southwest. The states with the largest Hispanic populations are California, followed by Texas, Arizona, Colorado, and New Mexico, but there are growing populations in the Northeast and Midwest as well (U.S. Census Bureau 2000b; see table 3). Politicians in the Northwest and Midwest must take these demographic shifts into consideration and include Mexican Americans as part of their political outreach.

Education remains an important area that needs improvement. Only one-quarter of Mexican Americans over twenty-five years of age has a high school diploma, and only 5 percent has a bachelor's degree. Among non-Hispanic whites in the same age range, 35 percent has a high school

Table 4 Employment patterns of Mexican Americans

EMPLOYMENT SECTOR	PERCENTAGE EMPLOYED
Operators, fabricators, and laborers	22.9
Technical, sales, and support	22.3
Service occupations	18.9
Managerial and professional	11.9
Precision production, craft, and repair	15.9
Farming, forestry, and fishing	8.0

Source: U.S. Census Bureau 2000b.

diploma, and 26 percent has at least some college education. Studies consistently demonstrate that individuals who are better educated are more likely to participate in electoral politics, which means that politicians will be held more accountable (García 2003).

It should come as no surprise given their average educational attainment that most Mexican Americans are not occupying high-paying professional jobs. Most are found in the service and labor sectors, which do not provide many opportunities for advancement, benefits, or mobility in the U.S. economy. Another correlate of **voter turnout** is type of employment: employees in the service sector are less likely to vote than are blue-collar workers, who typically participate in electoral politics. Tables 4 and 5 illustrate these factors.

Not surprisingly given their employment patterns, almost 25 percent of Mexican Americans live below the poverty line, compared to only 7.7 percent of non-Hispanic whites. The poverty rate is even higher for those under eighteen years of age, 31.5 percent. Low-income voters are less likely than other voters to be targeted by politicians and political parties. The result is that wealthier **constituents** are more likely to participate in political venues because they feel connected.

Various other factors influence the level of wealth for Mexican Americans, including size of family and average age. The average household size for U.S. families is 2.59, for Mexican American families it is 3.92. Mexican Americans are also younger than average. The average age for a Mexican American is twenty-five years old whereas the average age of the U.S. population is thirty-five years old. In short, because Mexican Americans

Table 5 Income brackets of Mexican Americans

INCOME RANGE	PERCENTAGE
$1–$2,499	1.8
$2,500–$4,999	1.6
$5,000–$9,999	7.1
$10,000–$14,999	10.0
$15,000–$19,999	10.5
$20,000–$24,999	9.7
$25,000–$34,999	16.1
$35,000–$49,999	16.7
$50,000–$74,999	15.9
$75,000 and over	10.4

Source: U.S. Census Bureau 2000b.

work very hard in low-paying jobs and have larger families to support, they tend to be poorer than the population at large.

The combination of these demographic characteristics may account for lower levels of voter turnout among the Mexican American population than among other groups who are on average wealthier, better educated, more proficient in English, and native born. Low voter turnout has led to a persistent perception that Mexican Americans are politically apathetic. In the following section I explore this perception further.

■ Mexican Americans and Political Apathy

One of the most dominant problems in the broader political realm, in my opinion, is apathy fueled by the all-too-common sense that one person can't make a difference. This problem is easily seen in low voter turnout, and in the disinterest and frustration voiced by every [wo]man. (Joyce L., 31)

Like Joyce, some might argue that Mexican Americans are politically apathetic or that their votes don't count. I would argue that political apathy is really a question of semantics. Do Mexican Americans participate in traditional electoral politics at the same rate as other ethnic groups? No. On other hand, if we include nontraditional outlets, such as grassroots organizing or local mobilizing strategies, then Mexican Americans as a whole are far from being politically apathetic and are powerful political players.

There are two reasons why Mexican Americans are seen as politically apathetic. The first is that research on political participation has typically focused on electoral politics, such as counting how many elected officials are of a particular race or **ethnicity,** or how many people in that group vote. The socio-demographics of Mexican Americans, including their age and level of education, decrease the overall numbers of Mexican Americans participating in electoral politics. The second reason Mexican American political participation has been overlooked is because it often falls outside the definitions of typical political behavior. For instance, some Mexican Americans and Mexican immigrants, particularly women, participate in grassroots political activism, activities that may not be assessed by researchers. Mexican American political participation may take such forms as community organizing for school reform, and key players may include non–U.S. citizens or those who do not speak English.

Mexican American participation in both electoral and nontraditional political outlets can be expected to increase, given the demographic projections. For instance, with regard to nontraditional political outlets such as grassroots organizing, the Mexican-origin population will continue to be fueled by newly arrived immigrants, resulting in a large portion of the population remaining young and without U.S citizenship. In traditional politics, the overall growth and sheer size of the population will result in more Mexican American elected officials and greater electoral turnout for initiatives, reforms, and political candidates (see figure 6).

■ Concluding Thoughts

Politics is pervasive in everything we do and in every position we take. Politics is closely tied to our ideology and is deeply psychological. The problem with politics is that many people, especially in the United States, believe that it is solely confined to partisan politics. And the deeper problem is that people believe they can live apolitical lives. (John L., 34)

As John notes, politics is part of everything we do. Even when we don't think we are being political, we are in fact making political decisions. This chapter has illustrated several reasons for lower levels of electoral participation among Mexican Americans that have little to do with political

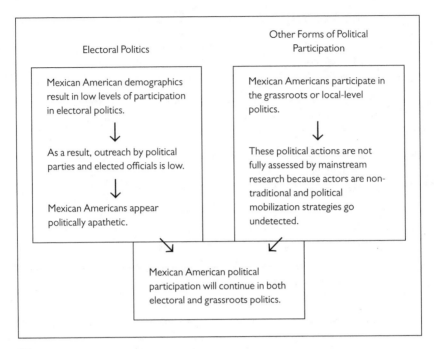

6. Forms of Mexican American political participation

apathy. It has also shown that the potential for Mexican American political participation, both traditional and nontraditional, is profound given the projected growth of this population.

There is great diversity within the Mexican American community. It is this diversity, however, that makes political **mobilization** strategies more difficult. That is, it is difficult for political leaders to determine which issues, agendas, and political platforms are particularly important for Mexican Americans and how they can target the group. The following chapters will explore in greater detail the answers to these issues, as well as how politics have played out in the Mexican American community.

■ Discussion Exercises

1. If you were trying to mobilize the Mexican American community, what demographic factors would you take into consideration?

2. Do you think labels are important for sustaining social movements?

3. What do you think is a more effective mode of political participation— electoral politics, such as supporting political campaigns or voting, or grass-roots mobilization?

4. Think about the various ways of describing Mexican Americans. How would you describe them?

■ Suggested Readings

Barrera, Mario. 1979. *Race and class in the Southwest: A theory of racial inequality.* Notre Dame, IN: University of Notre Dame Press.

Bedolla, Lisa Garcia. 2000. They and we: Identity, gender, and politics among Latino youth in Los Angeles. *Social Science Quarterly* 81 (1): 106–23.

Blea, Irene I. 1992. *La Chicana and the intersection of race, class, and gender.* New York: Praeger.

DeSipio, Louis. 1996. *Counting on the Latino vote: Latinos as a new electorate.* Charlottesville: University of Virginia Press.

García, F. Chris. 1974. *La causa política: A Chicano politics reader.* Notre Dame, IN: University of Notre Dame Press.

———. 1997. *Pursuing power: Latinos and the political system.* Notre Dame, IN: University of Notre Dame Press.

García, John A. 2003. *Latino politics in America: Community, culture, and interests.* Oxford: Rowman and Littlefield.

Gómez-Quiñones, Juan. 1994. *Roots of Chicano politics, 1600–1940.* Albuquerque: University of New Mexico Press.

Marquez, Benjamin. 1985. *Power and politics in a Chicano barrio: A study of mobilization efforts and community power in El Paso.* Lanham, MA: University Press of America.

———. 2003. *Constructing identities in Mexican American political organizations: Choosing issues, taking sides.* Austin: University of Texas Press.

Montejano, David, ed. 1999. *Chicano politics and society in the late twentieth century.* Austin: University of Texas Press.

Oboler, Suzanne. 1995. *Ethnic labels, Latino lives: Identity and the politics of (re)presentation in the United States.* Minneapolis: University of Minnesota Press.

Suro, Roberto. 1998. *Strangers among us: How Latino immigration is transforming America.* New York: Alfred A. Knopf.

Takaki, Ronald, ed. 1994. *From different shores: Perspectives on race and ethnicity in America.* New York: Oxford University Press.

Villarreal, Roberto, E., Norma G. Hernandez, and Howard D. Neighbor, eds. 1988. *Latino empowerment: Progress, problems, and prospects.* New York: Greenwood Press.

2

History of Mexican Americans
in Politics

Elected officials have historically been nonresponsive to Mexican American **constituents.** Most have been elected from **gerrymandered** districts, which have been designed deliberately to muffle political influence.
More recently, newly elected Mexican American political leaders have
enabled constituents to exert some appropriate civic action to better
articulate and express the needs for the community. It is still not enough.
Grassroots organizers, on the other hand, can be effective catalysts in
the public policy areas but they are often self-serving when it comes to
Mexican American constituencies. (Eduardo D., 63)

Eduardo's comments reflect the modern-day political culture of Mexican Americans. There is an overall feeling of dissatisfaction when it
comes to politics. Constituents feel that leaders overall are not responsive to Mexican American concerns and take the group for granted.
Starting from the Treaty of Guadalupe, in this chapter I explore the history
of both types of politics, electoral and grassroots, and how they are mani-
fested today in Mexican American political participation.

Mexican American Politics Takes Shape

The history of Mexican American political empowerment reflects coloni-
zation, occupation, and discrimination. The ancestors of today's Mexican
Americans were the mestizos, or mixed-blood descendants of the Spanish
conquerors and Mexican indigenous populations they came to subjugate
(see Martínez 1996). After independence, the Mexican government's suc-
cessive authoritarian regimes earned a reputation for mistreating the country's poor and uneducated **classes.** (Mexico's first truly democratic election
did not occur until the mid-1990s.) After the signing of the Treaty of
Guadalupe Hidalgo in 1848 ceded a large portion of northern Mexico to

the United States, Anglo settlers backed by the U.S. government continued to oppress the inhabitants of the region. As a consequence, Mexican American political participation in the U.S. Southwest has a long history of resistance against social and governmental persecution.

The history of Mexican American politics is traditionally divided into three major periods (Villarreal, Hernandez, and Neighbor 1988). The community's political **identity** began to take shape in the century following the 1848 U.S. annexation of 55 percent of Mexico's territory, including most of present-day Arizona, California, and New Mexico, as well as parts of Texas, Colorado, Nevada, and Utah. The **Chicano Movement** that sprang from the civil rights era of the 1960s and early 1970s marked the second significant period. And in the ensuing years, the third period, political participation has been characterized by both traditional and grass-roots **mobilization** strategies.

Mexico actually had little leverage in the negotiation of the Treaty of Guadalupe Hidalgo, because it had just lost the Mexican War. Following the signing of this document, Anglos soon migrated to the Southwest in search of land and other economic opportunities (see Barrera 1979). The region had a wealth of untapped resources. As the Anglo presence in the Southwest grew, so did its domination over most of the Mexican-origin people living there. It mattered little to most Anglo settlers that the region's existing inhabitants had been here for centuries—or as was the case for some Native American groups—thousands of years. Backed officially and tacitly by the government, including law enforcement officials, Anglo settlers began routinely to deny Mexican Americans their property, civil, and social rights supposedly guaranteed by the treaty. As the Anglo population grew, Mexican Americans were relegated to lower socio-political status. For instance, a dual wage system for Mexican and Mexican American workers became accepted and eventually institutionalized practice.

Following the U.S. annexation of Mexico's territory, early Anglo settlers unscrupulously took land from the rightful Mexican owners. Anglo pioneers were afforded property rights over those who were of Mexican origin. Mexicans were quick to organize in opposition to such actions. Joaquin Murieta, Gregoria Cortez, and Tiburcio Vasquez were considered some of the great champions of poor Mexicans living in the newly annexed United States (Castillo and Camarillo 1973). Joaquin Murieta, for instance, was forced by Anglos to leave his home when gold was discovered in the northern California region where he lived. Murieta established a reputation as a "murdering bandit" in the Anglo community and as a revered hero, albeit feared, in the Mexican community.

The original colonial land grants consisted of vast stretches of property, particularly along what had become the U.S.–Mexico border. Not surprisingly, much of this land was located along the fertile banks of the Rio Grande, which stretches from the mountains of New Mexico to Brownsville, Texas, where the river dumps into the Gulf of Mexico.

In New Mexico, Las Gorras Blancas, a group of local Mexican Americans, opposed Anglo encroachment on their lands in the 1890s. Most victims of land grabbers were poor New Mexicans unable to present their cases in the courts, and in any case the U.S. courts typically decided in favor of the Anglo squatters. Las Gorras Blancas responded by organizing grassroots opposition to unfair land acquisition. As a result of their actions, land rights of poor New Mexicans were recognized and confirmed in parts of the state.

The Mexican-origin community was also physically segregated. Laws were passed to limit the rights of Mexican Americans in schooling, housing, public gatherings, and even marriages to Anglos. Legal discrimination and widening poverty made social advancement increasingly difficult for the vast majority of Mexican Americans, as well as Mexican immigrants (see Acuña 1981). All the while, tensions between Mexican Americans and Anglos festered, sometimes erupting into violence, usually inflicted by Anglos against victims of Mexican origin (Gordon 1999; Sánchez 1993).

■ Effects of Immigration

Until the early 1900s, immigration from Mexico was virtually unrestricted. With few exceptions, people migrated north and south across the border with little difficulty. During the late nineteenth and early twentieth centuries, mutual aid societies began to flourish in Mexican-origin communities. These *mutualistas,* established to provide social support, were modeled after *sociedades mutualistas* prevalent among artisans and textile workers in Mexico. Politically, mutualistas provided networks for disseminating information on pressing issues as well as for organizing political opposition. The mutualistas founded at the beginning of the twentieth century helped set the stage for the creation of Mexican American organizations still functioning today.

In 1910, the Mexican Revolution provoked an enormous wave of Mexican migration (see topic highlight 1 for a profile of Mexican revolutionary leaders). Over the next decade, hundreds of thousands of Mexican citizens fled the violence and economic devastation caused by the war. Two hundred and fifty thousand Mexicans migrated to the United States. This

Topic Highlight 1. **Heroes of the Working Class**

Born in Morelos, Mexico, in 1879, Emiliano Zapata was a mestizo proud of his indigenous roots (see figure 7). He is often referred to as the father

■ 7. Emiliano Zapata (Courtesy of the Alma Alvarez-Smith private collection)

of Mexican activism. He was a strong advocate for community rights for his village, and he opposed President Porfirio Díaz's policies, which usurped land from poor peasants. He was arrested for his community advocacy in 1897 and later released. He continued to oppose the government and its abuses toward the poor, however. Part of Zapata's appeal was that he was bilingual in Spanish and Nahuatl and came from a modest background. As his popularity grew, Zapata formed his own revolutionary army, estimated at around five thousand men. Indicative of his growing power, he was supported by elected politicians and met with President Woodrow Wilson in 1915. He eventually drafted the Plan of Ayala, a declaration of independence proclaiming that land would be returned to the poor. He was killed in an ambush in 1919 in Morelos and is buried in Cuautla (Chávez Candelaria, García, and Aldama 2004; Keller 1994). His legacy as a revolutionary leader remained strong in both the United States and Mexico.

Another hero of the Mexican Revolution was Francisco "Pancho" Villa, born in 1878 in northern Mexico. He grew up as a peon on an *hacienda*. His reputation as a bandit began after he shot a wealthy landowner who had violated his sister. He gained a following as a freedom fighter and as a champion of poor people on both the sides of the border. In 1916 he led a raid on Columbus, New Mexico, retaliating against agrarian reforms and poor treatment afforded Mexicans. He was assassinated in 1923 by U.S. operatives (Chávez Candelaria, García, and Aldama 2004; Katz 1998). ■

wave of migration established the largest Mexican-origin communities in the Southwest.

■ The Great Depression

The Great Depression of the 1930s had the effect of reducing the Mexican-origin population. The unemployment rate during this period reached 25 percent. Given that wage earners at the time were almost exclusively men, this meant that approximately one of every four households did not have a breadwinner. Seeking a scapegoat for the nation's economic woes, President Herbert Hoover declared that Mexican immigrants took away American jobs and were partly responsible for the Depression (Gutiérrez 1995). Ironically, Hoover had recruited Mexican farmworkers during his tenure as head of the Allied relief operations during World War I.

During the Great Depression, the California legislature enacted a law making it illegal to hire Mexican immigrants. Over the next several years, extending into the Roosevelt administration, popular sentiment against Mexican nationals resulted in the continued deportation, forced and voluntary, of more than one-third of the Mexican community (Gutiérrez 1995). Although some Mexican immigrants voluntarily returned home because of the worsening U.S. economy, an estimated half million Mexican nationals and U.S. citizens of Mexican origin were involuntarily "repatriated." Incredibly, even more Mexican nationals and Mexican Americans would be deported in the 1950s.

■ World War II: A Catalyst for Change

The effects of World War II played a profound role in the development of Mexican American political identity (Ruíz 1998). Chicano servicemen, despite having earned the respect of their comrades in arms, continued to face poor and unequal treatment at home. Many of them decided it was time to fight back. World War II led to the formation of organized Mexican American interest groups. One of these was the League of United Latin American Citizens (LULAC), formed to promote greater political participation in electoral politics for Mexican Americans while fighting the discriminatory treatment they were receiving.

President Franklin Roosevelt signed the GI Bill into law in 1944. It, too, helped improve the lives of many Mexican American veterans and their families. The legislation provided financial assistance to help military veterans readjust to civilian life. Using these monies, many Mexican Americans purchased homes outside of barrios (predominantly Mexican neighborhoods) or attended college. Mexican American women who had worked outside the home during the war began challenging traditional female roles by forging new identities and paths for community leadership (Ruíz 1998).

■ The Zoot Suit Riots

By the mid-1940s, people of Mexican origin had become a major segment of the population of Los Angeles. As the country's involvement in World War II expanded, so too did the presence of mostly white military personnel in California. Those trends coincided with the rise of the pachuco culture among young, urban Chicanos. A culture clash soon developed between soldiers stationed in the region and the pachucos, also known as "zoot suiters," in reference to the wide-brimmed hats, high-waisted trousers, and broad-shouldered coats they wore. In the meantime, local newspapers began to write about a purported "Mexican crime wave" in the city. The reports, largely unfounded, sparked bitter animosity toward Mexican Americans.

In 1942, a twenty-two-year-old farmworker was murdered after a late-night party near the Sleepy Lagoon Reservoir. Ironically, the young man's death became the impetus for a Los Angeles Police Department crackdown that led to the arrests of hundreds of young Mexican Americans. Twenty-two Mexican American men and women were put on trial the following year in proceedings now widely condemned as a racially motivated perversion of justice. Seventeen of those charged were sent to prison, including twelve people convicted of murder—though the convictions were eventually overturned (see Escobar 1999).

During the ensuing months, tensions continued to grow between Mexican Americans and whites across Los Angeles. Several clashes occurred between military personnel stationed in the area and young Mexican Americans. On June 3, 1943, about two hundred sailors drove to East Los Angeles and began randomly attacking young Mexican Americans. Mobs of sailors and civilians participated in the assaults for days. Whereas a few token arrests of military personnel were made, hundreds of young Mexican Americans, most of whom were simply defending themselves or their property, were charged with rioting and vagrancy. To make matters worse, the *Los Angeles Times* and other local newspapers publicly praised the sailors for their actions. When First Lady Eleanor Roosevelt criticized the assaults by the soldiers, she was condemned for her comments.[1] Historians maintain that this event shaped the political identity of Mexican Americans because the riots brought national attention to their situation and meant they could no longer be ignored.

■ The Bracero Program

Economists had predicted widespread unemployment after World War II. Instead of labor surpluses after World War II, however, the postwar economy expanded rapidly, producing a substantial shortage of workers in the United States. To meet this labor shortage, the United States and Mexico instituted a contracted worker system called the **Bracero Program** in 1942. This initiative allowed agricultural employers in the United States to recruit and hire low-cost Mexican labor on a seasonal basis. Mexican laborers were granted temporary worker status on a season-by-season basis. Unfortunately, employers had wide discretion over pay as well as working and living conditions for the immigrant workers (Calavita 1992).

Critics have described the Bracero Program as a virtual slave labor system because of its legacy of widespread worker and human rights abuses. To avoid the substandard labor conditions often endured by the braceros, many immigrants sidestepped the program and entered the country illegally in search of employment. The strong U.S. economy during this period further fueled the growth of the Mexican-origin community. As a result of slumps in the economy and subsequent labor surpluses, the program ended in the early 1960s (Calavita 1992).

Operation Wetback

An economic recession in the early 1950s again turned popular sentiment against Mexican immigrants and heightened discrimination against Mexican Americans. Beginning in 1954, the **Immigration and Naturalization Service** (INS) began expelling Mexican nationals, many of whom were in the country legally, in a program known as Operation Wetback. Apprehensions and deportations reached 1,300,000 that year, according to the INS. During the next five years, approximately 3.8 million Mexican nationals were deported (Gutiérrez 1995). This operation marked one of the darkest periods of anti-Mexican sentiment in U.S. history. Nevertheless, illegal immigration continued throughout the 1950s, further fueling growth of the Mexican-origin community and the U.S. economy.

With the diversification of the U.S. economy in the 1950s, a growing number of undocumented immigrants pursued higher-paying, urban-based jobs in the manufacturing and industrial sectors. The U.S. steel industry in the Midwest attracted thousands of Mexican immigrants to cities like Chicago, Illinois, and Hammond and Gary, Indiana. Mexican Americans also relocated to urban areas in pursuit of better paying jobs (Moore and Pachon 1985). It was during this period that the Mexican-origin population began its shift from rural areas to the urban communities where they are predominantly located today.

◼ The Beginnings of Political Outreach to Mexican Americans

Modifications in U.S. immigration law in the 1960s also affected the growth of the Mexican-origin community and its political influence. For instance, the 1965 **Immigration Act** lifted restrictions that had previously barred the admission of many immigrants and created a system of family preference, making it easier for families to reunite in the United States (Magaña 2003). As the Mexican-origin population grew, the number of eligible voters in the community reached the critical mass needed to influence national elections. The 1960 Kennedy-Nixon presidential race turned out to be one of the closest contests in history. Realizing the uphill fight it had against Republican candidate Richard M. Nixon, the Democratic Party launched its first significant campaign to recruit Mexican American voters. The effort featured Democratic presidential nominee John F. Kennedy's "Viva Kennedy" campaign. Local Mexican American politicians were called upon to stump on behalf of and with Kennedy himself (see Moore and Pachon 1985). The national campaign also made use of the candidate's wife, Jacqueline Kennedy, who spoke fluent Spanish. The family's Catholic background, which didn't sit well with a significant proportion of Protestant voters, appealed to many Mexican American voters, most of whom were Catholic.

The **War on Poverty** and **Great Society** programs, initiatives of the Lyndon B. Johnson administration in the 1960s, were created to eradicate poverty. These efforts included job training, housing assistance, environmental cleanup, and educational support systems. These approaches to diminishing poverty solidified Mexican American support for the Democratic Party.

◼ The Voting Rights Act

The **Civil Rights Movement** sought to secure rights that had been promised but never delivered to African Americans under the U.S. Constitution, such as freedom of expression, equal education, and fair access to the opportunities afforded to Anglos. The **Voting Rights Act** of 1965 (VRA) was passed during this period, further expanding the Mexican American community's political clout. The act was designed to eliminate official and unofficial barriers created specifically to discourage people of color from participating in the political process. Before the VRA was enacted, Mexican Americans and other minorities faced a wide array of obstacles to voting, including poll taxes and literacy and language tests. Mexican American voters were also physically intimidated, threatened, and sometimes beaten when they sought to register to vote or participate in routine political activities. The VRA prohibited voting and election practices that discriminated on the basis of race or color (see de la Garza and DeSipio 1997). This included abuses of the redistricting process such as gerrymandering, the process of redrawing the boundaries of political districts to favor a particular political party or to isolate minority voters to minimize their influence.

The VRA also allowed Mexican Americans to challenge the use of **at-large voting** systems. In at-large voting, all the voters in a city or county may vote for all candidates, even those who do not represent their ward or district. In comparison to **district voting**, this system deters full political participation by poor and minority voters. For instance, it favors experienced candidates with significant financial resources as well as those who appeal to mainstream Anglo values rather the specific interests of minority groups. As a result, candidates from wealthier areas continued to be reelected. The VRA did not guarantee that minorities would control districts but it did ensure that minority choices would not be defeated by white block voting or gerrymandered election schemes.

In 1982, the VRA was amended to protect language minorities: Spanish speakers, Asian and Pacific Islanders, Native Americans, Alaskan natives, and Aleuts. In communities with more than a 5 percent language minority of voting age, ballots and other voting materials were required to be made available in the minority language. These language minorities were protected because their history of discrimination in education directly resulted in low voter registration rates. Moreover, language was a particularly effective way of deterring minority political participation (Polinard 1994).

The VRA has afforded many opportunities for Mexican American participation in the political process. Unlike other minorities, however, the Mexican-origin population is still faced with a unique problem that cannot be easily remedied by the VRA, namely the large number of immigrants in the community. This means that despite the obstacles to political participation that were removed by the VRA, the simple fact remains that Mexicans resident in the United States cannot vote because they are not U.S. citizens (de la Garza and DeSipio 1994).

■ The Chicano Movement

The political tumult of the 1960s also marked the birth of the Chicano Movement. Author Roberto Rodriguez (1996, 1) called the movement "a civil and human rights struggle." Inspired in part by the victories of the black Civil Rights Movement and aided by the passage of the Civil Rights Act of 1964 and the VRA of 1965, the Chicano Movement galvanized Mexican Americans throughout the nation. The movement helped spawn hundreds of organizations nationwide, including the **United Farm Workers of America** (UFW) union, **La Raza Unida** Party (LRU), La Alianza de Pueblos Libres, the Brown Berets, The National Chicano Moratorium, The Crusade for Justice, the Mexican American Youth Organization, and Movimiento Estudiantil Chicano de Aztlán (MEChA).

Whereas church-based organizations had served as a wellspring of civil rights activity for African Americans, universities would become the intellectual and spiritual stronghold of the Chicano Movement (Rodriguez 1996). By the 1960s, Mexican Americans had begun to reap the rewards of educational advancement made possible by the GI Bill, with a growing number acquiring college degrees. A key demand of the movement's leadership was the establishment of more opportunities in higher education. **Chicano** studies and **Latino** studies programs in universities nationwide are part of the legacy of that movement.

The Chicano Movement championed several major objectives: labor rights (especially for nonunionized farmworkers); an end to segregation, discrimination, and political repression; restoration of land grants to their owners in border states throughout the Southwest; and increased educational opportunities for students of Mexican origin in public schools, colleges, and universities. Although it has been argued that the Chicano Movement originated in the post–World War II efforts for Mexican American self-determination, it was not until the 1960s that the movement became notably politicized. Until then, most Mexican American leaders were willing to work within **traditional politics** (that is, electoral politics) to achieve their goals. The 1960s counterculture trends and a push for equal rights by many in the U.S. population inspired Chicano leaders to flex their political muscle (Rodriguez 1996).

Most researchers credit the birth of the Chicano Movement to the activism of Reies López Tijerina, who led an effort to reclaim New Mexico's colonial-era land grants in 1966 and 1967. Tijerina wanted the federal government to honor the promises it made under the Treaty of Guadalupe Hidalgo that the descendants of Spanish land grant recipients would retain the rights to their property.

The Chicano Movement took another step forward under the leadership of Rodolfo "Corky" Gonzales in Denver, Colorado. As founder of the Crusade for Justice, Gonzales helped articulate what it meant to be a Chicano in his epic poem "I Am Joaquin." Gonzales would go on to play a major role in the LRU (Moore and Pachon 1985).

The Chicano Movement's nationalistic overtones were reflected in its idealization of the Mexican American community's ancestral links to the indigenous culture of the ancient Aztecs and the mythic paradise of Aztlán. Some argued that Aztlán was located somewhere in what is now the U.S. Southwest and that the Mexican-origin population of the region resided in land unjustly occupied by an imperial aggressor, namely the United States. This philosophy was articulated in a document called "El Plan Espiritual de Aztlán" presented at a 1969 Youth Conference in Denver.

In 1963, Mexican Americans in Crystal City, Texas, organized against the Anglo-dominated city council. With the support of Chicano activists this political organization developed into the LRU, formed in 1970 in Crystal City (García 1989). This was the first and only political party organized specifically to represent Mexican Americans. The LRU reached its zenith between 1972 and 1974, when it sponsored candidates for governor of Texas, among other offices.

This party generated unprecedented support for Chicano platforms, such as increasing Chicano/a political representation at the local and state levels, enacting educational and bilingual reforms, and ending institutionalized segregation. The party achieved significant success in Texas and established a handful of strongholds in California and New Mexico.

Eventually the LRU lost momentum and membership. Among its weaknesses were that women were relegated to subordinate positions and relatively powerless roles. They eventually created their own caucus within the party, but many women felt that their needs and desires were virtually ignored. Bitter debates as to how the party should be led and what sort of agenda should be supported resulted in internal tensions and the LRU's ultimate demise. Furthering the disintegration of the party, several leaders in the party left to start their own organizations, whose initiatives were pushed forward by the passage of the VRA. Others simply concluded that

Topic Highlight 2. César Chávez

Best known as the founder of the UFW and as a champion of social justice, César Chávez was born in 1927 in Yuma, Arizona. Chávez's legacy as a leader was influenced by his childhood experiences. For instance, his mother and grandmother instilled the values of spirituality as well as empathy toward the needy. His family turned to farm labor after losing their property during the Depression. At ten years old, Chávez's experience as a migrant worker made him aware of the injustices of field labor as well as this group's lack of political voice to fight violations and abuses. Chávez opposed the poor working conditions of migrant laborers, including lack of electricity, running water, or bathroom facilities. It was also apparent that workers were being exposed to unsafe and hazardous working conditions and that workers continued to be underpaid. Despite his traveling as a migrant laborer, Chávez eventually graduated from school and joined the Navy for four years. He became a self-educated man, immersing himself in readings on nonviolent social change, labor history, social activism, and unions. He was also influenced by the writings of Saint Francis of Assisi and Mahatma Gandhi.

Chávez began his activist career as a community organizer in California during the 1950s. He started working at the Community Service Organization, a Latino outreach agency. He eventually branched off to form the National Farm Workers Association in 1962. With a focus on fighting for social justice, the National Farm Workers adopted the slogan "Viva La Causa" (long live the cause). The organization would later unite with the Filipino labor union AWOC to become the United Farm Workers Organizing Committee (UFWOC), eventually known as the UFW. In 1965, Chávez led a strike against the California wine grape growers seeking to improve working conditions for migrant workers. In 1966, Chávez led a 340-mile march from Delano to Sacramento, California, to bring attention to the strike. The march, consisting of approximately five thousand participants, culminated in the grape industry agreeing to consider the strikers' demands. Unionization, however, was out of the question, so Chávez reasoned that he could bring greater national attention to the plight of farmworkers by calling for a lettuce boycott. Chávez continued to support the principle of nonviolence even though strikers were intimidated and beaten. In 1968, Chávez fasted publicly in order to bring more attention to the strike as well as to convince his colleagues of the virtue of nonviolent protest. These fasts brought media attention to the farmworkers as well as public support from other civil rights leaders, such as Martin Luther King Jr. and Robert Kennedy. In 1970, the boycott ended and union contracts were eventually signed. Later Chávez's social activism shifted to fighting the unsafe use of pesticides and the hazards this poses for workers as well as the environment.

Chávez died in 1993, but his work continues to be honored even after his death. In 1994, President Bill Clinton posthumously awarded him the Presidential Medal of Freedom. Some states have declared a holiday in his name.[2] ■

working within the two established political parties would benefit Latinos more in the long run.

Another important component of the Chicano Movement was the farmworkers' struggle launched by civil rights activists César Chávez and Dolores Huerta in the early 1960s (see topic highlight 2 for a profile of Chávez). In 1965, the UFW led a strike against grape growers in the California community of Delano. The Agricultural Workers Organizing Committee (AWOC), a Filipino union, launched the strike. The AWOC leadership had asked César Chávez to help organize the strike because so many of the farm laborers by then were Mexican or Mexican American. The strike and boycott, which lasted several years, eventually resulted in the unionization of migrant workers as well as improved working conditions and higher wages.

The Los Angeles school walkouts of 1968 proved to be another pivotal event in the Chicano Movement. Triggered by the cancellation of a play deemed inappropriate for students at Wilson High School because of its political content, the walkout soon spread to other predominantly Mexican American schools in the city. By week's end, the protest included thousands of students, whose leaders used the event to dramatize their discontent with the poor quality of education afforded Mexican American students. Among their demands were greater cultural sensitivity, access to bilingual education, improved facilities, and better teachers.

◼ Mexican American Political Organizations

> Organizations do help out Mexican Americans, but is such help a good thing? I do not know. I have mixed feelings about this. On the one hand certain organizations help us out by empowering us as individuals, but on the other hand no leader has recently come from any organization revolving on Mexican Americans. What good is a group if it cannot empower its members to reach the national scene? (Jose A., 22)

Political organizations have played key roles in empowering the Mexican American community at the local, state, and federal levels, through litigation, advocacy, and support programs. These organizations illustrate the power of local politics and mobilization. Some of the most visible political organizations today include the National Association of Latino Elected and Appointed Officials (NALEO), the National Council of La Raza (NCLR), the League of United Latin American Citizens (LULAC), and the Mexican American Legal Defense and Education Fund (MALDEF). More recently, **lobbying** groups that represent individuals from Mexico and the United States collectively have been becoming important political watchdogs for immigrants living in the United States.

Although ostensibly these organizations are nonpartisan, they have maintained strong ties with the Democratic Party. These organizations provide a variety of services for the community, including lobbying elected officials, providing research on topics of concern, disseminating information to the community, litigating on behalf of the abused, and offering social services.

League of United Latin American Citizens

LULAC, originally called United Latin American Citizens, is the largest and oldest **Hispanic** advocacy organization in the United States. In 2003, the group claimed more than 115,000 members in all fifty states, Puerto Rico, and Guam. Founded in 1929, the group was born in an era when "No Mexicans Allowed" signs were still commonplace at parks, restaurants, and other public spaces throughout the Southwest (LULAC; Texas State Historical Association).

LULAC is dedicated to the advancement of the Mexican American community and sponsors projects to improve their economic, educational, and public health conditions. LULAC was founded through the merger of four 1920s-era Texas-based Mexican American community groups: the Knights of America, the Corpus Christi Council of the Order of the Sons of America, the Alice Council of the Order of the Sons of America, and the League of Latin American Citizens. The latter had invited the Order of the Sons and the Knights of America to one of its events in Harlingen, Texas, on August 14, 1927. During the meeting, a proposal was put forth to unite the groups. When a key organizer proposed that the new organization allow only U.S. citizens as members, a protest ensued and most of those in attendance left the meeting.

On February 17, 1929, twenty-five delegates and several dozen supporters looked on as a resolution was passed formally uniting the four groups. The resolution declared that the organization would work to assist Mexican Americans (that is, U.S. citizens) living throughout Texas, Arizona, New Mexico, and California. Three months later, the first LULAC convention was convened in the Texas coastal town of Corpus Christi.

In the early years of the group, LULAC members and recruiters often operated at great personal risk to their jobs, positions in the community, and even their physical well-being. In some cases, LULAC officials were accused of having communist sympathies simply for having gathered to discuss public policies directed toward Mexican Americans. In the 1940s, the Federal Bureau of Investigation ordered LULAC officials placed under surveillance.

The organization also attracted suspicion in its own community. Some felt insulted by the organization's rule that members be U.S. citizens. Critics viewed the restriction as proof that LULAC was more interested in assimilation into white mainstream culture than in helping the entire Latino community. Despite those obstacles, LULAC's membership soon spread to Arizona, Colorado, New Mexico, and California. The organization was also opened to noncitizens as well as citizens.

Among the organization's major achievements, LULAC financed the lawsuit *Del Rio Independent School District v. Salvatierra*. This was the first class-action suit to oppose the policy of segregated Mexican schools in Texas. In 1948, the U.S. District Court, Western District of Texas, ruled in a separate case, *Delgado v. Bastrop Independent School District,* that separate schools for children of Mexican descent violated the Constitution. It would not be until the 1960s that Texas schools would be fully integrated.

Today, LULAC is among the leading groups in the country working to protect the civil rights of Mexican Americans, while also working closely with other communities of color. A nonprofit organization, LULAC has more than six hundred councils in communities across the country. Along with their other activities, LULAC councils award scholarships every year; conduct citizenship classes and voter registration drives; develop affordable housing, youth training, and adult leadership training; and lead grassroots advocacy work.

Mexican American Legal Defense and Education Fund

MALDEF addresses the ever-changing needs of the Latino community, concentrating its efforts in the following areas: employment, education, immigration, access, language, and equity issues. Founded in the 1960s, MALDEF began its work in the state of Texas during the civil rights era. Its initial focus was on developing programs and policies that would encourage Mexican American student participation, including bilingual education, scholarships, and desegregation attempts.

In 1966, a pivotal event would redirect the organization's efforts. A Mexican American woman lost her leg in a work-related accident. MALDEF believed that the woman deserved a settlement for the company's negligence. The issue was taken to court but the jury that was to decide the case was all Anglo and was challenged as unlikely to give the woman a fair trial. The judge agreed and placed two Spanish-surnamed jurors on the jury. Indicative of the poor treatment of Mexican Americans in the 1960s judicial system, one of the two people named to the jury had been deceased for ten years and the other was a noncitizen. MALDEF was determined to mount a major battle to end discriminatory jury selection practices in Texas and to improve the treatment of Mexican Americans in the judicial system.

Challenging long-standing judicial practices would require substantial funding. In 1967, members of MALDEF met with the Ford Foundation to outline the overall problems that were confronting Mexican Americans in the Southwest. The Ford Foundation granted MALDEF a sum of $2.2 million for civil rights litigation and $250,000 for scholarships to be disseminated to Mexican American law students. This grant established the organization and many of the principles it still practices today.

In terms of education, a variety of legal challenges by MALDEF throughout the Southwest led to many changes within the public school system. Until the 1960s, for instance, Anglo students were able to transfer out of classes that were predominantly Mexican American. As a result of MALDEF-sponsored litigation, school testing was determined to be inherently biased against students whose primary language was not English or who came from lower socioeconomic backgrounds. The Texas system of school funding was also ruled discriminatory because it was based primarily on property taxes. Predominantly Mexican American districts, being poorer, generated less property tax revenue than Anglo districts, and the schools were correspondingly underfunded. Student textbooks also depicted Mexican Americans in a negative light. MALDEF successfully challenged all of these practices and was able to improve how Mexican American children learned.

It was not uncommon at the time for Mexican Americans to be denied promotions and advancements in their employment simply because they were not Anglo. Employers would subject Mexican American employees to unfair requirements for promotion, thus successfully keeping Mexican Americans in lower positions in the workforce. Furthermore, Mexican Americans who filed complaints of job discrimination risked being terminated. MALDEF ensured certain rights and privileges for Mexican Americans in the workforce. The organization worked to monitor employers and bring litigation against those employers who discriminated against employees simply because of their **ethnicity.**

In the 1960s, as a result of the VRA and MALDEF litigation, many Mexican Americans were incorporated into the electoral system. For instance, MALDEF challenged policies that required Mexican American voters to register annually. The organization also challenged at-large voting schemes and districts that were reapportioned in discriminatory ways. The language of ballots was also challenged. MALDEF was highly successful at increasing the overall number of Mexican American voters, particularly in the Southwest.

Some of MALDEF's greatest recent successes have been in immigration. MALDEF worked to overturn California's **Proposition 187,** which would have ended education services to the state's undocumented immigrants. MALDEF also has challenged federal policies that place unfair burdens on Latino immigrants seeking admission into the United States. For instance, MALDEF lobbied for the Nicaraguan Adjustment and Central American Relief Act (NACARA), which protects refugee immigrants living in the United States from deportation.

National Council of La Raza

The NCLR, established in 1968, serves to eradicate poverty and discrimination. In order to accomplish these goals, the NCLR directs its efforts in four ways. First, the agency's capacity building initiative serves to support Mexican American community-based organizations that facilitate needs locally. Second, the NCLR conducts research and policy analyses for Latinos. Third, the organization supports and conducts research on projects that may affect Latinos domestically. Finally, it is very successful at public outreach and information, particularly in the media.

The organization's policy think tank, the Policy Analysis Center, located in Washington, DC, has an excellent reputation for research. The center provides both primary and secondary research on such issues as immigration, education, housing, poverty, civil rights, foreign policy, and special populations. It has provided expert testimony on issues related to the Mexican-origin community, such as immigration, education, free trade, race relations, health policy, and tax reform, to name but a few. The NCLR also works in conjunction with other organizations to carry out comprehensive and related projects and initiatives. Another way it assists Mexican Americans is through its use of "issue networks," which channel funding to HIV/AIDS, health, education, and leadership initiatives.

Finally, the NCLR promotion of positive images in the media has been perhaps one of its most successful programs. It funds a series of important content analysis studies that have examined the number and types of Latino characters in the media. Finally, the organization rewards individuals who have worked toward establishing a positive image of Latinos.

National Association of Latino Elected and Appointed Officials

NALEO is a nonprofit and nonpartisan group whose mission is to promote the election and appointment of Latino public officials. The group's members are appointed and elected politicians, civil servants, and other public officials. The number of appointed and elected public officials across the country grew nearly 30 percent between 1984 and 2002 to 4,464.

NALEO touts itself as the leading national organization of Latino political empowerment. Its mission statement reads, "Our membership forms a network of leaders throughout the United States dedicated to raising the level of Latino participation in the decisions that affect us all" (NALEO Educational Fund). The group holds an annual conference and coordinates the planning and operation of NALEO Institutes across the country. These institutes are intensive hands-on training workshops aimed at teaching community leaders and aspiring politicians how to run a political campaign or grassroots lobbying effort. The organization also operates the NALEO Educational Fund, which includes citizenship projects, youth and adult training programs, education outreach projects, and research on public policy and electoral issues that affect Latinos.

■ Binational Organizations

The number of individuals from Mexico living in the United States has increased dramatically over the last three decades. They are a force that can no longer be ignored. Their mounting **demographic** presence has given them political and economic clout that must be reckoned with on both sides of the border. Economists estimate that remittances, monies sent home from Mexicans working abroad, are the third largest source of revenue, after oil and manufacturing, in Mexico. Furthermore, dual nationality, a status granted since the early 1990s, allows Mexican nationals to purchase property and retain certain voting privileges in Mexico even after they become **naturalized** U.S. citizens. Mexican immigrants living in the United States provide a net gain to the Mexican economy through remittances.

Lobbying organizations that are **binational** in focus have become important political agents for the Mexican-origin community. Recently, the Mexican Foreign Ministry created a council of one hundred Mexicans living in the United States to advise the government on the needs and policy concerns of Mexicans living there. Members of this organization, most of them born in Mexico, are described as vocal advocates for Mexicans in the United States. Immigration reforms, civil rights, and unfair treatment toward Mexican immigrants are just some of the platforms these lobbying organizations address.

The Institute of Mexicans Abroad coordinates programs for the millions of Mexicans who live in the United States (*Houston Chronicle,* 12/19/02). The organization was created as a watchdog agency to address the mistreatment of Mexicans living in the United States. These organizational directives address the fact that Mexican nationals are here to stay, should be treated fairly, and should not be ignored.

Because millions of Mexicans travel home over the holidays, in 1990 the **Paisano,** or **Compatriot, Program** was designed to ease travel between the

United States and Mexico (*Houston Chronicle* 11/26/96). Mexican Consulate offices provide information on travel regulations, such as necessary documents for produce exceptions (for importing fruits or vegetables), transportation procedures, taxes, and car insurance.

In short, the growing presence of Mexican nationals in the United States means that organizations have to take on the needs of a growing binational community. More recent efforts to address immigration reform, language use at the worksite, and immigrant extradition cases have taken on greater importance for organizations like MALDEF and the NCLR. This trend will no doubt continue.

■ The Effect of Political Organizations

In general, Latino political organizations have become much more prominent in combating both electoral and grassroots discrimination. Today these organizations play key advocacy roles at the state, local, and federal levels, as well as in electoral and grassroots politics. However, the need for Mexican Americans to support these organizations cannot be underestimated. As Paul notes, understanding and supporting these organizations further solidifies Mexican American political identity:

> I think organizations like LULAC, MEChA, and MALDEF do in fact try to do the best for all of us. I think sometimes we are still left out by others, but for the most part, it appears these groups really try to fight for equality. More and more so, people of my generation and younger are not very clear on these organizations and don't really understand what they do and what they stand for, which is sad because that is when we start to lose the unity and the actual purpose/missions of these organizations. I think if the education of individuals continues, focusing on the fact that these organizations are out there to help us out, we can become stronger and stronger. I honestly believe if we got more involved, our organizations could become as strong if not stronger than the NAACP, which represents African American citizens. (Paul Q., 27)

■ Concluding Thoughts

This chapter reviewed some of the major events that led to the Mexican American community's political activism. Mexican Americans have confronted discrimination throughout their history in the United States. U.S. history is replete with cases of segregation and barriers set up to discourage electoral participation. Past abuses have shaped the Mexican American community into one that is politically responsive, confronting issues at the federal, state, and local levels.

The history of Mexican American politics can be divided into several major periods. The first period of political activism began after the U.S. annexation of the Southwest. With the growth of the newly created Mexican American community as well as the continued migration of Mexicans northward, a Mexican American political identity began to flourish. Mutual aid societies grew in Mexican-origin communities to provide social support for people marginalized between two cultures. Many of these societies set the stage for political organizing in contemporary times.

The Chicano Movement marked another significant period. Many political agendas, such as land rights, segregation, educational reform, farmworkers' rights, and basic civil rights reforms emerged during this period. Many leaders came out of the movement, including César Chávez, Dolores Huerta, Corky Gonzales, and Reies López Tijerina.

Congress approved the VRA in 1965, which eliminated many of the barriers that discouraged minority political participation. It set the stage for various reforms to promote participation in electoral politics by people of color. The VRA eliminated blatantly discriminatory practices such as biased redistricting, at-large voting, and gerrymandering. The VRA encouraged Mexican American electoral participation, but many in the Mexican-origin population cannot vote because they are not American citizens.

Political organizations became much more prominent in combating both electoral and grassroots discrimination. Today, these organizations play key advocacy roles at the state, local, and federal levels, as well as in electoral and grassroots politics. No longer can Mexican American organizations focus only on issues specific to the United States. They must also expand their agendas to include a binational focus that incorporates the United States and Mexico.

The increase in Mexican American political participation today is attributed to several factors. First is the overall growth of the population. Second, historians contend that the Chicano Movement politicized many leaders who are today active in both electoral and grassroots politics. Third, the passage of the VRA resulted in fuller and more meaningful

Mexican American political participation in both traditional and nontraditional political outlets.

■ Discussion Exercises

1. What are the factors that consistently mobilize the Mexican American community?

2. What seem to be the major historical moments that solidified Mexican American political participation?

3. What were some of the agendas of the Chicano Movement?

4. Which of the issues that mobilized the Chicano Movement are still relevant today?

5. Why are political organizations such as MALDEF, NCLR, and LULAC important agents for change?

6. Can you think of other important political organizations? What are their political agendas?

■ Suggested Readings

Acosta, Teresa Polomo. 2003. *Las tejanas: 300 years of history.* Austin: University of Texas Press.

Carroll, Patrick James. 2003. *Felix Longoria's wake: Bereavement, racism, and the rise of Mexican American activism.* Austin: University of Texas Press.

De León, Arnoldo. 2001. *Ethnicity in the sunbelt: Mexican Americans in Houston.* College Station: Texas A&M University Press.

García, F. Chris. 1974. *La causa política: A Chicano politics reader.* Notre Dame, IN: University of Notre Dame Press.

García, Mario T. 1994. *Memories of Chicano history: The life and narrative of Bert Corona.* Latinos in American Society and Culture No. 2. Berkeley: University of California Press.

Grofman, Bernard, and Chandler Davidson, eds. 1992. *Controversies in minority voting: The Voting Rights Act in perspective.* Washington, DC: Brookings Institution.

Gutierrez, José Angel. 1998. *The making of a Chicano militant: Lessons from Cristal.* Madison: University of Wisconsin Press.

Marquez, Benjamin. 1993. *LULAC: The evolution of a Mexican American political organization.* Austin: University of Texas Press.

——. 2003. *Constructing identities in Mexican American political organizations: Choosing issues, taking sides.* Austin: University of Texas Press.

Muñoz, Carlos Jr. 1989. *Youth, identity, power: The Chicano Movement.* New York: Verso.

Navarro, Armando. 1995. *Mexican American Youth Organization: Avant-garde of the Chicano Movement in Texas.* Austin: University of Texas Press.

——. 1998. *The Cristal experiment: A Chicano struggle for community control.* Madison: University of Wisconsin Press.

——. 2000. *La Raza Unida party: A Chicano challenge to the U.S. two-party dictatorship.* Philadelphia: Temple University Press.

Niemann, Yolanda Flores, ed. 2002. *Chicana leadership: The frontiers reader.* Lincoln: University of Nebraska Press.

Shockley, John S. 1974. *Chicano revolt in a Texas town.* Notre Dame, IN: University of Notre Dame Press.

◾ Notes

1. There is an excellent website covering the whole Zoot Suit Riots at http://www .pbs.org/wgbh/amex/zoot/eng'filmmore/webcredits.html. It includes text, music, pictures, letters, and other valuable archival materials.

2. For more information on Chávez's life and work, read *Elegy on the death of César Chávez* (Anaya 2000) and Chavez's entry in the *Encyclopedia of Latino popular culture in the United States* (Chávez Candelaria, García, and Aldama 2004).

3

Elected Officials and Party Affiliations

Elected officials do not meet the needs of Mexican Americans; they merely are meeting the needs of the wealthy people who control the system. Even elected officials who are Mexican Americans are subjected to the corruption within the system so therefore those officials become puppets of the puppet master. (Joaquin L., 23)

This century has seen a large increase in the number of Mexican Americans, yet we have not seen a commensurate rise in political power. Are some groups just better at manipulating power for their own interests? And if so, how can Mexican Americans be better at controlling power for their benefit? This chapter examines electoral participation and party affiliations of Mexican Americans and why their level of power has not yet coincided with the overall growth of the population. Several factors influence Mexican American political participation, such as the level of outreach by political parties and elected officials, the socioeconomic characteristics of the population, and key issues that drive **mobilization.**

Recent census data as well as outreach by the Republican and Democratic parties illustrate the growing political importance of Mexican Americans in elections. Because most of the data on political behavior focus on all **Latino** groups as a whole, also examined in this chapter are the political attitudes and party affiliations of other Latino groups, such as Cubans, Puerto Ricans, and Central Americans. Although Mexican Americans do not have a level of power corresponding to the size of their population, Latinos in general have made significant political inroads.

Factors in Political Participation

Several **demographic** factors contribute to low levels of electoral participation among Mexican Americans. First, a substantial proportion of the Mexican-origin population is made up of immigrants; approximately 40 percent of the population is foreign born. As discussed in chapter 1, individuals who are not U.S. citizens are not necessarily apolitical, but they cannot vote.

Voter age is also a factor. There is a strong correlation between age and **voter turnout,** in that older people are more likely to vote and to be interested in issues such as housing, education, and taxes. Voting is a way to affect the outcome of these agendas. Mexican Americans are on average younger than other ethnic or racial groups, such as Anglos. The median age of the Mexican American population is twenty-five, compared to thirty-four for non–Mexican Americans. Two reasons account for the younger median age. First, Mexican Americans tend to have larger families, so that children bring down the average age. Second, immigrants tend to be younger; given that they make up a large percentage of the community, the population can be expected to remain young. That said, the Mexican American population is growing rapidly and is aging, making them an increasingly desirable group for political outreach.

Another reason Mexican Americans are sometimes overlooked in electoral politics is that they tend to be poorer and have less education relative to other groups, particularly Anglos. The 2000 census data indicate that 25 percent of Latinos live under the poverty line compared to 11.1 percent of non–Mexican Americans, and that one out of three Latinos aged twenty-five and older has less than a ninth-grade education. In general, white middle- and upper-**class** homeowners tend to be much more involved in politics (Magaña and Short 2002).

 Political Agendas

Politicians shape their agendas to meet the needs of those who vote (Magaña and Short 2002). For instance, elected officials know that senior citizens are very likely to vote because on average they are older, wealthier, and have time to hold their elected officials accountable. The American Association of Retired Persons (AARP) is perhaps one of the most powerful **lobbying** forces in Washington, DC. Is it any surprise that political campaigns routinely focus on social security reform and subsidized prescriptions?

Agendas that address the needs of Mexican Americans rarely carry the same political clout. The lack of outreach on the part of elected officials is also indicative of the complex and not easily categorized Mexican American agenda. In the last decade, however, immigration reform, **affirmative action,**

Table 6 Reasons why Latinos become U.S. citizens

REASON	PERCENTAGE CITING
U.S. citizenship allows you to vote in U.S. elections.	95
U.S. citizenship provides opportunities for your children.	90
U.S. citizenship helps your relatives to immigrate to the United States.	88
U.S. citizenship offers you more protection under the law.	87
U.S. citizenship enables your children to become citizens.	85
U.S. citizenship makes you eligible for government programs.	85
U.S. citizenship helps you get a better job.	84
U.S. citizenship allows you to participate in American life.	83
U.S. citizenship makes your life better overall.	82
U.S. citizenship helps you earn more money.	69

Source: NALEO National Latino Immigrant Survey, 1989.

and bilingual education have all served to rally Mexican Americans in un-precedented numbers. Research indicates that when Mexican Americans are targeted, they will participate in electoral politics (Moore and Pachon 1985). Other studies indicate that **naturalized** Mexican Americans have higher than average levels of political participation. One study found that on average 75 percent of people who are registered vote, whereas 86 percent of those who are naturalized and registered will vote (Synovate Research 2002).

Naturalization

Not surprisingly, political parties set up voter registration booths outside locations where new citizens have just been naturalized (de la Garza and DeSipio 1997). In a NALEO study, researchers asked Latinos why they chose to become naturalized U.S. citizens. Respondents overwhelmingly indicated that their reason was their desire to vote (see table 6).

Political Apathy

Mexican Americans have been labeled as politically apathetic or as not concerned with being "real Americans." One activist remarked, "If Anglos are apathetic when it comes to voting, Latinos are even more so because many have one foot here and the other in their country of origin. But we need them here and now" ("Hispanics Seek Power" 1995). This statement is partly true because it speaks to the large number of Latinos who are immigrants and because it addresses the fact that voter apathy is a nation-wide phenomenon.

In an article examining minorities and political apathy in California, one political pollster described the process as playing out in several ways. The first and most prevalent type of voter apathy is a pattern whereby older, wealthier Anglos tend to vote and other citizens avoid politics. The remaining apathetic voters are individuals who are not content with the system and feel their vote will not make a difference (Yoachum 1994). Vera is an example of the second type of voter, who maintains that her vote does not matter and politicians are out of touch:

> There is no trust in the system, and because we have ancestors from Mexico they are afraid that if they say anything against the government they will be deported. Elected officials do not know the community or our needs. They have to live in the community and understand what is going on to truly represent us. (Vera G., 56)

Perhaps the following numerical breakdown can shed some light on patterns of voter apathy. In the 1994 election in California, 26 percent of the adult population in California was identified as Latino. However, the number of Latinos actually eligible to vote totaled only 14 percent of the population. In the end only 8 percent of the voters who actually cast ballots in the election were Latino (Yoachum 1994).

■ Party Preference

Party preference is strongly correlated with socialization. That is, a person who is raised in a household of Democrats is likely to register as a Democrat. Furthermore, if the majority of elected officials in the community where one resides belong to a particular party, residents are more likely to choose that party. This is the case in Texas, where the Republican Party has a strong influence on voters and former Governor George Bush had relative success wooing Mexican American voters. As a result, Texas has a slightly higher than average percentage of Mexican Americans who vote Republican. Party choice is also based on ideological preference. A person may prefer a party because of its stance on social or ethical issues, such as government spending, the death sentence, or abortion, to name but a few.

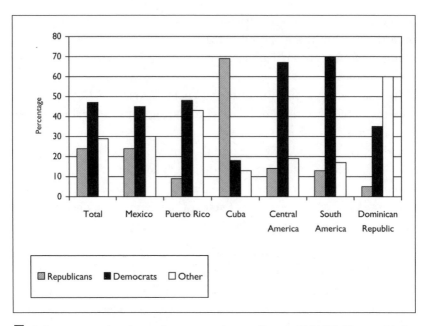

8. Latino party identification by country of origin (Source: 2004 U.S. Hispanic Market Report, Synovate, Inc.)

The Republican Party in recent years has stepped up its recruitment efforts in the Latino community, aware of the overall growth of the population as well as the fact that recent immigrants tend to be more **conservative,** particularly on social issues. Although the percentages have shifted slightly in recent years (see figure 8), the 1989–1990 Latino National Political Survey found that 71 percent of Puerto Ricans and 67 percent of Mexican Americans identified themselves as Democrats or leaning toward the Democratic Party; in contrast, 69 percent of Cuban Americans identified themselves as Republicans (de la Garza, Falcon, García, and García 1998).

In the 2000 presidential election, Latinos as a group voted two to one for Democrat Al Gore over Republican George Bush. Overall, 48.4 percent of the total population voted for Al Gore, whereas 63.7 percent of the Latino population did so. On the Republican side, 47.8 of the total population but only 33.3 percent of Latinos voted for George Bush. A mere 3.8 percent of the total population and 3.0 percent of Latinos voted for Ralph Nader. Preliminary analysis of the returns from the 2004 election indicate that the Republicans continue to gain ground among Latino voters. Nationally, the

Table 7 Party affiliations of Latinos in selected major cities in 2002 and 2004

PARTY AFFILIATION	LOS ANGELES	NEW YORK	CHICAGO	MIAMI	HOUSTON	DALLAS	SAN FRANCISCO	SAN ANTONIO
2002								
Democrat (%)	71	57	47	24	47	34	69	41
Republican (%)	22	17	13	56	27	25	8	15
Other (%)	7	26	40	20	27	41	24	44
2004								
Democrat (%)	45	56	54	25	44	36	58	52
Republican (%)	27	14	15	55	21	31	17	17
Other (%)	27	30	31	21	35	33	25	31

Source: Synovate Research 2004.

percentage of Latinos who voted for George Bush in 2004 increased about 5 percent compared to the 2000 election. Table 7 shows the percentages of Latinos in eight major U.S. cities identifying themselves as Republicans and Democrats. Interestingly, between 2002 and 2004, the percentage of Latinos identifying themselves as Democrats increased slightly in Chicago and San Antonio, but decreased in Los Angeles, Dallas, and San Francisco. Party identification remained virtually the same in Miami.

▌ Partisanship and Latinos

Mexican Americans have historically made up the largest proportion of U.S. Latinos. Yet population growth as well as social and economic advances among other Latino groups have generated political gains overall for U.S. Latinos. The other Latino groups, such as Cubans, Puerto Ricans, and Central Americans, have different histories, resulting in patterns of political participation that are different from that of Mexican Americans. For instance, because Cubans entered the United States as refugees rather than as immigrants, their political interests and partisanship differ from those of Mexican Americans. Puerto Ricans are more similar to Mexican Americans in their voting patterns because Puerto Rico is near the United States and they have been recruited for labor needs. It is important to highlight these inter-group differences because Latinos are often categorized as a single block, particularly with regard to political agendas (see topic highlight 3).

Topic Highlight 3. Histories and Partisanship of Non–Mexican American Latino Groups

Although politicians often treat Latinos as a monolithic interest group, Latino subgroups vary markedly in their histories and consequent political leanings, as this topic highlight shows. (South Americans, although part of the Latino population, are not profiled here because their numbers are small and little information specific to them is available.)

■ Puerto Ricans

Puerto Rico was ceded to the United States as a result of the Spanish-American War in 1898. Natives of the island were granted U.S. citizenship in 1916, and the island became a U.S. commonwealth in 1952. Puerto Rican migration into the United States over the years, especially in recent decades, has generated political clout nationwide, particularly in New York, New Jersey, Illinois, and south Florida. The Puerto Rican community's affiliation with the Democratic Party can be traced back to the population's U.S. roots in Democratic strongholds such as New York and Chicago. Until recently, the Democratic Party was the only major party conducting significant voter outreach efforts among Latinos, including Puerto Ricans. Additionally, the island's inhabitants have benefited greatly from public welfare programs developed largely by congressional Democrats.

The Democratic Party has been much more supportive than Republicans on issues of interest to Puerto Ricans, such as granting the island greater autonomy and providing public assistance. During the Clinton administration, the president agreed to an eventual cessation of U.S. military training exercises on the island of Vieques, Puerto Rico. Residents there complained that bombing and beach assault exercises by the Navy and Marines had polluted the environment and reduced tourism. Republican leaders in Congress wanted the training exercises to continue, but the president eventually ordered the military to withdraw its forces and train elsewhere. The move was viewed as an acknowledgment of the growth in Latino political clout.

Cubans

Major migration by Cubans to the United States began after the 1959 revolution led by Fidel Castro. In short, the Castro government declared itself an ally of the Communist Soviet Union. As a result, pro-capitalist Cubans began moving to the United States. Castro soon solidified his authoritarian grip on power in Cuba, prompting an even greater exodus of his island's citizenry.

In the 1960s, a major surge of Cuban migration occurred. More than 275,000 Cuban refugees came to the United States, virtually tripling the existing Cuban American population. Subsequent waves of Cuban migration have substantially increased Cuban American clout in Miami and other areas of south Florida, as well as New Jersey. From a party affiliation perspective, however, the 1960s are the most important period. When Cubans arrived in the United States, their concerns were centered on foreign policy and how the United States would deal with Fidel Castro and his regime. The Republican Party espoused a tough stance against Castro's regime, forging a strong relationship between Cubans and Republicans. Cuban American enmity toward most Democrats was cemented by the actions of President John F. Kennedy, whom Cuban exiles blame for the failed invasion of Cuba at the Bay of Pigs in 1961. In 1966, President Lyndon B. Johnson signed the Cuban Adjustment Act, allowing Cuban immigrants arriving in the United States, legally or not, to quickly gain permanent legal residency status. Even so, Johnson received little political support among Cubans.

Angry that Castro has remained in power for more than forty years, Cuban Americans have focused their political energy on foreign policy and the U.S. government's dealings with Castro. As with other groups of Latino voters, not all Cuban Americans vote Republican. A growing number of second- and third-generation Cuban Americans have begun to take a more moderate stand on U.S. foreign policy toward Cuba. For instance, some Cuban Americans have requested a loosening of travel restrictions so that they can visit Cuba, as well as opening of trade between the two countries, policies that are more in line with the Democratic platform.

■ Central Americans

The arrival of substantial numbers of Central Americans in the United States occurred comparatively recently. Most of that migration has occurred as a result of socially and economically devastating wars in the region, especially during the 1980s. Large numbers of Nicaraguans, Salvadorans, and Guatemalans fled to the United States, many seeking political asylum. The patterns of political participation for Central Americans and their party affiliation differ somewhat from those of other Latino groups. Although there are few studies on voter turnout and political affiliation among Central Americans, they, too, do not vote monolithically. Regional affiliation seems to play a substantial role in the voting patterns of these citizens. For instance, voters living on the West Coast and in Washington, DC, tend to vote for Democrats whereas those in other regions, such as Florida, often vote Republican. ■

■ Mexican Americans and Party Politics

The Democrats, especially, will be the political party to help Mexican Americans. But the Democrats have to take over the leadership from conservative Republicans like Bush, and then I see the future looking brighter. (Christine M.)

Historically, federal government policies helped solidify Latinos' party preference. Franklin D. Roosevelt's **New Deal** implemented programs and policies that assisted both Mexican Americans and Puerto Ricans. Federal housing, urban development, and employment programs strengthened the affinity among Mexican Americans for the Democratic Party, which was further cemented in the 1960s when the **Great Society** and **War on Poverty** programs (under President Lyndon B. Johnson) implemented public works, medical assistance, and job training programs.

Another pivotal event strengthening the union between Mexican Americans and the Democratic Party was the Viva Kennedy campaign in the early 1960s. Designed to highlight issues that were attractive to Mexican Americans, the campaign was one of the first to mobilize Mexican American voters. Examples of specifically tailored platforms and issues were improved education and better working standards. The Kennedy campaign also ran ads in Spanish. The impressive turnout, and the proportion of Mexican Americans who supported Kennedy, have been partly attributed to this campaign's specific outreach. For instance, in some Texas precincts, Mexican American voter turnout for John F. Kennedy was around 80 percent. As mentioned previously, Kennedy was also the first Roman Catholic elected to the U.S. presidency. The overwhelming majority of Latino voters in the 1960s were Roman Catholic.

After the passage of the **VRA** in 1965, minority political participation grew in both proportion and numbers. During the 1960s, however, disillusionment with the political mobilization and empowerment strategies of major political parties escalated within the Mexican American community. Furthermore, Mexican American activists felt that the major political parties failed to consider their special needs and took Mexican American voters for granted. As described in chapter 2, this led to the founding of the short-lived **LRU** (see García 1989).

In general, Mexican Americans are still Democrats, although in recent years their support for the party has diminished slightly. For a growing number of Mexican Americans, the Republican agenda on issues such as family values and abortion has resonated. In addition, Mexican American voters, like other Americans, increasingly identify themselves as Independents. Alternative political parties, such as the Green Party, have also made modest inroads into the Latino community, particularly among the more educated.

Recent attempts by the Republican Party to recruit Mexican Americans have entailed changes in policies and rhetoric. For instance, in the 1996 presidential election, Republican politicians and candidates touted tougher restrictions on immigration, an agenda unlikely to appeal to Mexican Americans. When former California Governor Pete Wilson ran for president as a Republican in 1996, he maintained that hundreds of thousands of immigrants come to the United States to utilize social services or welfare. Standing in front of the Statue of Liberty he said, "The illegal immigrants are coming, and that means crime, more welfare mothers, and lotsa spicy food!" (Nyhan 1995). This statement is not only racist, but simply untrue, as undocumented immigrants are not eligible for social services. In contrast, Democrats by and large have not made immigration a political agenda because of the party's long-standing relationship with Mexican Americans (García 1997).

I see Democrats as the party that tries to make an effort to meet the needs of Mexican Americans, whereas Republicans are only trying to use us for a vote. (Vera G., 56)

During the 2000 presidential election, the Republican Party sought to overcome the reputation of being anti-immigrant and consequently anti-Latino. Several reasons may account for this reversal. The anti-immigrant sentiment that characterized the mid- to late 1990s mobilized the Latino population. After the passage of anti-immigrant legislation in California, for example, Mexican Americans mobilized to counter attacks on affirmative action and bilingual education. Furthermore, some Mexican Americans who were naturalized in response to anti-immigrant sentiment were now voting **constituents** who had not forgotten the anti-immigrant rhetoric of the Republican Party. Furthermore, newly released census data indicate that Latinos are the fastest growing group in the country; recent projections indicate that by 2008 there will be an estimated 18.7 million eligible **Hispanic** voters, almost twice as many as there were in 1998 (10.6 million; see figure 9).

One scholar astutely noted the absence of certain issues in the Republican Party platform during the 2000 election—including immigration, bilingual education, English only, militarization of the border, and restricting access to social services—and suggested that the Republican Party made its position on these issues more generic in order to ensure a broader appeal to all constituents (García 2003). Another indication of the growing Mexican American population is that during the 2000 election both political parties produced Spanish-language commercials. Playing on family values, one Republican television commercial depicted a Latino family having a barbecue. A young male in the group described how he no longer felt content with the Democratic Party and perhaps it was time for a change of party. Other commercials depicted the Republican Party as in line with the Mexican American values of hard work and the need to protect families. The presidential candidates explicitly conveyed their affinity toward the Latino community, using the occasional Spanish word or pointing out the commonalities they possessed.

For the 2004 presidential election, Democratic candidate John Kerry spent an estimated one million dollars to air Spanish-language television advertisements in states with growing Latino populations: Florida, New

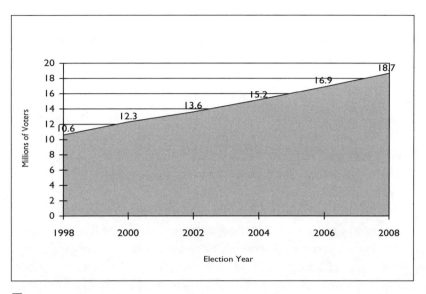

■ 9. Projected increase in Hispanic eligible voters, 1998–2008 (Source: 2004 U.S. Hispanic Market Report, Synovate, Inc.)

Mexico, Nevada, Arizona, Colorado, Ohio, Oregon, Washington, Pennsylania, and North Carolina. The thirty-second ads highlighted honor, such as respect for family, the military, and the working people. Incumbent President Bush's ads targeted toward Latinos illustrated Kerry's lack of commitment to Latino issues, illustrated in his pro-choice stance.

■ Conservative or Liberal: What Are Mexican Americans?

A recent survey by the Pew Hispanic Center indicates that the political views of Mexican Americans are not easily categorized and can be defined as both **liberal** and conservative. As evidence, almost 50 percent believe abortion should be illegal and 46 percent feel that having a child without being married is unacceptable. These findings are counterbalanced by the fact that a significant proportion of the respondents believed in big government and immigration proposals in order to assist individuals who need help. What these findings mean is that Mexican Americans cannot be easily categorized. They are not a group with clear, distinct interests and, therefore, cannot be mobilized easily by one political party or the other.

Yet, the researchers concluded that the Republican Party has a ripe opportunity to recruit Latinos because of their social conservatism and because Latino loyalty to the Democratic Party is currently low (Roeser 2003).

Latino Elected Officials

> Too often the leaders make promises, but when it comes to making positions in their office or helping people, they soon forget about Mexicans voting. Even when the various Latino caucuses meet to investigate or request certain changes, Mexicans have been ignored.
>
> When people become involved in any **grassroots** organization, they can become empowered and changes can occur. However, it is only when the objectives are clear and people are well organized that changes occur. The leaders of those groups have to be elected by group members and not self-appointed or assume the position of leader. (Virginia P., 62)

Over the last forty years there has been a significant rise in the number of Latino elected officials at the federal level (see topic highlight 4). According to the *National Directory of Latino Elected Officials* (NALEO 2003), in 2003 there were 22 U.S. representatives (no U.S. senators), 10 state executive officials, 61 state senators, and 160 state representatives. The overwhelming majority of Latino elected officials are found in local rather than state or federal elected positions. In 2003 there were 474 county officials, 1,585 municipal representatives, 638 judicial and law enforcement representatives, 1,723 school board officials, and 180 special district officials, bringing the total number of Latino elected officials to 4,835. Of this number, 1,427 were Latina. Overall, however, the number of Latino elected and appointed officials is still scant in comparison to the forty million Latinos living in the United States. The party affiliations of these officials reflect Latinos' longstanding association with the Democratic Party: 1,460 identified themselves as Democrats and 122 as Republicans, 1,504 defined themselves as holding nonpartisan offices, 12 defined themselves as Independents, and 1,755 did not indicate their party affiliation.

Do Latino Elected Officials Make a Difference?

There is some interesting and possibly surprising research on whether the presence of Latino elected officials at the federal level makes a difference

Topic Highlight 4. Prominent Mexican American Federal Elected Officials

The biographies of three U.S. congressmen—Henry B. Gonzales (D-TX), Edward R. Roybal (D-CA), and Ed Pastor (D-AZ)—illustrate the political advances of the Mexican American people.

 Henry B. Gonzales

Henry B. Gonzales was the first Texan of Mexican descent elected to the U.S. Congress, serving from 1961 to 1998. Born in San Antonio in 1916, Gonzales was the son of a former mayor of Mapimi, Durango, Mexico. His parents instilled in him the value of political service. He attended the University of Texas and later Saint Mary's University Law School. In 1950, he began his political career by running for the Texas House of Representatives, supported by the Mexican American and African American communities. He describes feeling discouraged when he was told that no Mexican American could ever win an election in an Anglo community. He narrowly lost this first election by 2,000 votes.

He continued his efforts in politics, running for a position on the San Antonio City Council. He won, becoming the first Mexican American ever to win a seat on the council, which was ironic given that San Antonio is predominately Mexican American. His tenure as a councilman was characterized by his strong commitment and devotion to desegregation and civil rights reform.

In 1956, he became the first Mexican American Texas state senator, serving two terms. With the support of John F. Kennedy, he ran for the U.S. Congress in 1960. Although his reelection campaigns were always hard-fought, he remained a congressman for thirty-seven years. He died in 2000. (For more information about Gonzales, see Chávez Candelaria, García, and Aldama 2004; Gómez-Quiñones 1990).

 Edward R. Roybal

Former Congressman Edward R. Roybal was one of the Mexican American community's political pioneers. Roybal served in the U.S. Congress from 1963 to 1993, the first Mexican American elected to the U.S.

House from California since the 1870s. The growing Mexican American population in Los Angeles in the wake of World War II opened the way for more Mexican Americans to gain a foothold in local government. A longtime community activist, Roybal was elected to the Los Angeles City Council in 1949 and served as a councilman until 1962, when he ran for Congress. Representative Roybal penned the first bilingual education bill in 1967. He also formed a committee to improve education, housing, and employment opportunities for Latinos nationwide. This committee also helped Latinos obtain appointments to federal jobs, government commissions, and the like. Roybal also helped create the Congressional Hispanic Caucus in 1976 and its nonprofit research and educational wing, the Congressional Hispanic Caucus Institute. The caucus continues to assist Latinos in Congress pool their power base (Library of Congress).

■ Ed Pastor

An Arizona native, Ed Pastor was born in the mining community of Claypool. He graduated from Arizona State University (ASU) with a

■ 10. Congressman Ed Pastor

bachelor of arts degree in chemistry in 1966 and earned his Juris Doctor (law degree) from ASU in 1974. Pastor was elected to the Maricopa County Board of Supervisors in 1976 and went on to serve three more terms before resigning in May 1991 to run for the U.S. Congress. The first Mexican American to represent the state of Arizona in the U.S. Congress, Representative Pastor has served thirteen years and is still in Congress as of the writing of this book (see figure 10). As of 2004, he serves on the House Appropriations Committee and on several sub-committees: the Subcommittee of Energy and Water Development; the Subcommittee of Transportation, Treasury, Postal Service, and General Government; and the Subcommittee on the District of Columbia. During the 104th Congress, Congressman Pastor was chairman of the Congressional Hispanic Caucus, of which he remains an active member. He also was named by the Democratic leadership to the party's eight-member Leadership Advisory Group. (Chávez Candelaria, García, and Aldama 2004; United States House of Representatives). ■

for Latinos. It shows that Latino elected officials in Congress have no direct or substantive influence on policies that affect Latinos. Their voting stance tends to be similar to those of other members of Congress and closely related to their party affiliation (Hero and Tolbert 1997).

Ethnicity and politics are intimately intertwined and influence each other. When a candidate of color runs for office, can he or she ever be seen as anything but an ethnic candidate? The person may not explicitly link political agendas or aspirations to his or her ethnicity but may always be perceived to do so. Furthermore, an ethnic candidate may also be viewed with suspicion by the culture he or she represents, which may ask if this candidate truly represents the needs of that community. Mexican American candidates and elected officials are held to at least two levels of scrutiny, that of the culture at large and that of the culture they represent (Hero and Tolbert 1997). Ana's comment reflects the common mistrust of Mexican American politicians:

Mexican American politicians break their promises. And this happens because they don't trust each other; the problem is in their human nature, and the fact that no commitments are respected. (Ana C., 19)

The influence of Latino officeholders is felt more strongly at the local level. Studies have confirmed that Latino elected officials at the local or county level are more likely to support initiatives of interest to Latinos. Locally elected Latinos have brought greater attention to Latino issues, set relevant policy agendas, increased the number of minority hires, and paved the way for other minority elected officials.

Harry Pachon, president of the Tomás Rivera Policy Institute, maintains that power for the Latino population is found not only in the ranks of elected officials but also among bureaucrats and appointed officials who have a significant influence on the outcome of critical public policy decision making:

Overall it seems that increased Latino representation in public policy-making bodies does have a favorable impact on policies which are helpful to the political community. In any case, the *lack* of Latino representation has not proven to improve the conditions of Latinos in the United States. Given this dismal record, one can argue that the burden of proof falls upon these agencies in documenting how they have been, and continue to be, responsive to the Hispanic community lacking any Hispanic representatives themselves. (Pachon 1983)

▪ Concluding Thoughts

Because Latinos are voting in greater numbers, political parties are paying increasing attention to their potential voting power. In Texas and California, these voters can mean the difference between winning or losing an election. Political parties must make sure they run candidates who will represent Mexican American interests, and the Democratic Party can no longer take these voters for granted. On the other hand, this chapter has illustrated that the numbers of elected Latino officials are not commensurate with the numbers of Latinos, and specifically Mexican Americans, in the general population.

Clearly the community is complex and cannot be easily described or categorized. This makes targeting these voters difficult. Survey evidence reveals that the values of Latinos cut across conservative (pro life) and liberal (more government spending) ends of the political pendulum. More-over, various Latino subgroups, such as Cubans, Puerto Ricans, and Cen-tral and South Americans, have different patterns of party affiliation based on their history as well as their positions on various issues.

Several factors influence Mexican American political participation, in-cluding the level of outreach by political parties and elected officials, the socioeconomic characteristics of the population, and key issues that drive mobilization. Given all the demographic projections, Latinos have to be better incorporated into electoral politics in upcoming years. Increasing the numbers of potential voters among all groups in the United States is in the best interest of every citizen, not just Latinos. As Jennifer notes,

I believe that there will be an increase of pandering by both political parties not only to Mexican Americans, but to Cubans, Puerto Ricans, South Americans, and other groups of this nature, because their population is growing by leaps and bounds. The states that will be most affected by the future of politics for this group, however, are states that share a border with Mexico, like Arizona, New Mexico, and Texas. (Jennifer D., 22)

■ Discussion Exercises

1. How should Mexican American politics be defined? Who should be targeted (U.S. born or a **coalition** of first- and second-generation Mexican Americans or also those of Central/South American, Cuban, or Puerto Rican origin) and why?

2. What should be the goals of Mexican American politics in community set-tings and why?

3. What should be the goals of Latino politics?

4. How do Mexican American interests overlap with and differ from those of other groups (such as Anglos, African Americans, Asians)? What accounts for these similarities and differences?

5. Would you prefer to see more Mexican American politicians at the local or the national level? Why?

6. Do you think elected officials meet the needs of Mexican Americans? Why or why not?

7. What recommendations would you make to improve Mexican American electoral participation? How do you see the changes playing out?

8. How should political parties pay better attention to Mexican Americans?

9. What strategies should political parties use to recruit and retain Mexican American voters?

■ Suggested Readings

de la Garza, Rodolfo O., Louis DeSipio, F. Chris García, John A. García, and Angelo Falcon. 1992. *Latino voices: Mexican, Puerto Rican, and Cuban perspectives on American politics.* Boulder, CO: Westview Press.

DeSipio, Louis. 1996. *Counting on the Latino vote: Latinos as a new electorate.* Charlottesville: University of Virginia Press.

García, John A. 2003. *Latino politics in America: Community, culture, and interests.* Oxford: Rowman and Littlefield.

Hamamoto, Darrell Y., and Rodolfo D. Torres. 1997. *New American destinies: A reader in contemporary Asian and Latino immigration.* New York: Routledge.

Menjívar, Cecilia. 2000. *Fragmented ties: Salvadoran immigrant networks in America.* Berkeley: University of California Press.

Schneider, Anne, and Helen Ingram. 1993. Social construction of target populations: Implications for politics and policy. *American Political Science Review* 87(2): 334–46.

Solis, Julie, Elizabeth R. Forsyth, and David Lopez-Lee. 1990. One voice, one future: A Latino funding agenda from the Latino community and its leadership. The Los Angeles County Latino assessment study (LACLAS). Summary report. Los Angeles: Tomás Rivera Policy Institute.

4

Mexican American Women and Politics

I wish there were more Latina elected officials. All you ever see is the same Anglo male elected official. If there were more Latinas, I think there would be more attention given to Latinas and their needs. (Grace N., 46)

This chapter examines the presence of Mexican American women in elected office at the federal, state, and local levels, as well the motivating factors that sustain their participation. Also explored is the presence of Mexican American women in **grassroots** political movements. Research on Mexican American women, and women of color in general, shows that their participation in grassroots politics is innovative and effective. Their political behavior is not fully assessed, however, because their actions fall outside of traditional classifications of politics, and often these women do not define themselves as "political." Mexican-origin women are minorities in politics and they are nontraditional political actors, in that many do not speak English and are not U.S. citizens. Because much of the research focuses on Latinas in general, not Mexican-origin women specifically, in several locations I describe Latina political behavior.

■ Female Elected Officials

During the past forty years, the number of Latinas participating in electoral politics has grown substantially. Numerous factors contribute to this trend including unprecedented outreach by political parties and elected officials and the increasing importance of the expanding **Latino** population. However, the majority of Latino politicians remain men. One factor contributing to this gender gap may be cultural, in that Latinas have traditionally been expected to conform to traditional female gender roles. Running for political office has not been a common trend or legacy. A Latina candidate, like women candidates generally, may still be viewed as unusual.

According to the Center for American Women and Politics (CAWP), there are fourteen women of all races (14 percent) in the U.S. Senate (CAWP, "Facts"). In 2004, of the 535 congressional seats, women held 74 (13.8 percent). At the state level, women held 81 of 315 elective executive-branch positions (25.7 percent). Of the 7,382 state legislators, 1,659 (22.5 percent) were women, breaking down as follows: 411 of 1,971 state senate seats (20.9 percent) and 1,248 of 5,411 of the state house seats (23.1 percent). CAWP reports that the number of females serving in state legislative positions has increased more than fourfold since 1969. The states with the highest percentages of women in their legislatures were Washington (36.7 percent), Maryland (34.0 percent), Colorado (34.0 percent), Vermont (31.1 percent), New Mexico and California (both 30.0 percent), Connecticut (29.4 percent), Delaware (29.0 percent), Oregon (28.9 percent), and Nevada (28.6 percent).

Of the seventy-four women in the U.S. Congress in 2004, eighteen (24.4 percent) were women of color. African American women and Caribbean American women served as delegates to the House of Representatives from the District of Columbia and the Virgin Islands. Of the eighty-one women serving in statewide executive-branch elective offices, five (6.2 percent) were women of color. Women of color constituted 18.4 percent of state legislators, with 85 senators and 221 representatives. All but eighteen of the female elected officials surveyed were Democrats (CAWP, "Facts").

■ Latina Elected Officials

The numbers of Latina elected officials are also promising and growing substantially. As of 2003 NALEO had 1,427 Latina elected and appointed officials in its registry (NALEO 2001). There were seven Latinas in the U.S. Congress. At the state level, there were three Latinas in state executive positions, and there were sixty-one at the state legislative level.

Latinas are represented in greater numbers at the local and county levels than at federal or state levels. In 2003, 167 Latinas held county positions, 150 Latinas were in judicial and law enforcement positions, and 335 Latinas held elective municipal offices. There were 605 Latinas serving on school boards, and a few were superintendents. Latina political participation is significant in Arizona, California, Colorado, Illinois, New Jersey, New Mexico, and New York, states with large Latino populations.

■ Why They Run

A study focusing on 150 Chicana/Latina elected representatives in California investigated the characteristics of Chicana/Latina elected officials (Takash 1993). Most of the respondents had graduated from college, with either a bachelor's or a master's degree, and most hailed from working-class backgrounds. They identified their fathers' occupations "as laborers, construction workers, gardeners, and agricultural workers; their mothers' occupations as housewives or service sector workers" (422). In line with their working-class backgrounds, common political agendas or interests focused on poverty and economic reform issues. Most of the respondents had experienced significant economic and social mobility, with family incomes of between $50,000 and $100,000. Most of the Chicana elected officials were born in the United States and defined themselves as Catholic, and 82 percent identified themselves as Democrats. (See topic highlight 5 for a profile of one Chicana elected official.)

Surprisingly, more than half of the respondents stated that their political role models were not women. When asked about the most important event, factor, or influence leading them to run for office the first time, the Mexican American women cited dissatisfaction with politics or the incumbents. The remaining respondents claimed a general concern with social change.

In terms of political experience, these women had never held elective or appointed positions, and more than half indicated they had never worked for political campaigns. Consistent with the experiences of many Mexican American elected officials, these women did say they had worked at the community level as a starting point of their political careers. Almost half said they had gained valuable experiences in women's organizations. The top two organizations in which these elected officials had participated were the National Women's Political Caucus and the National Organization of Women (Takash 1993). Another study confirmed the importance of political organizations, such as the Comisión Femenil Mexicana Nacional, the National Hispana Leadership Institute, MALDEF, and the **Hispanic** Steering Committee of the National Women's Political Caucus, as stepping-stones for political office (Montoya, Hardy-Fanta, and García 2000).

CAWP has created a web page that focuses on the growing number of Latina elected officials (CAWP, "Elección"). This information confirms

Topic Highlight 5. **Lucille Roybal-Allard**

Congresswomen Lucille Roybal-Allard began her political career as a member of the California State Assembly for three terms (United States House of Representatives). Born and raised in Boyle Heights, California, she is the eldest daughter of Lucille Beserra Roybal and retired Congressman Edward R. Roybal, who served as a member of Congress for thirty years. She graduated from California State University, Los Angeles, is married to Edward T. Allard III, and is the mother of two adult children (see figure 11).

■ 11. Congresswoman Lucille Roybal-Allard

Lucille Roybal-Allard is the first Mexican American woman to be elected to the U.S. Congress, and the first Latina to be appointed to the House Appropriations Committee, perhaps one of the most powerful committees in Congress. Her other committee appointments oversee funding for small business development, international trade, the 2000 census, national security, labor relations, law enforcement, equal employment issues, and the restructuring of the INS.

In 1999, she became the first woman elected to chair the Congressional Hispanic Caucus. In this position, she focused on education, economic development, and access to health care. Roybal-Allard was also elected chairwoman of the California Democratic Congressional Delegation. She became the first woman, the first Latina, and the first member ever to assume this position through an election, rather than just being given the position based on her seniority. ■

that most elected officials are college graduates, have experienced socioeconomic mobility, are nominally Catholic, and come from working-class backgrounds. Most of the women also become involved in politics through a desire to mobilize change at the community level. Interestingly, perhaps because of the lack of female elected officials, most of the respondents stated that their role models were men.

Mexican American women are also personally committed to politics at a macro as well as micro level. As Joyce notes,

> I define politics on two levels. One level is personal conviction; this level is the foundation for the ways that I perceive the broader political realm. A personal political framework includes commitment to the groups one has investment in and strong beliefs in how those groups and individuals within those groups should be treated by and within social institutions. The second level, then, includes support and involvement with groups or individuals with power to take social action, make changes, make a public difference. Exercise of personal politics is daily, and that daily personal action should be reflected in involvement on this second level. Broader political involvement can range from the simple and necessary act of informed voting to involvement on the local level through volunteer work with church and civic groups geared toward social action and reform to writing letters to state government leaders and actively contributing, financially or otherwise, to a specific political party. (Joyce L., 31)

■ Political Attitudes and Expectations

The National Latino Political Survey surveyed Latinas and Latinos regarding the issues they were concerned with as **constituents** (de la Garza et al. 1998). This was perhaps the first political survey that identified the differences between Latinos and Latinas as well as among Cuban, Mexican, and Puerto Rican constituents. Questions addressed a variety of attitudes, such as whether men or women were more capable in public office during a crisis. The majority of respondents did not voice a strong opinion, but there were some important group differences. Mexican and Puerto Rican women were more likely to answer "women," whereas Mexican and Puerto Rican men were more likely to answer "men." Cuban male and female respondents alike were more likely to indicate that men were better suited than women to be in positions of political power during a crisis; clearly for them gender is an important feature in politics.

What do women generally and Latinas specifically expect from their elected officials? In a recent survey conducted by the League of Women Voters (LWV), women overall saw the necessity for reform and political action in the area of social issues. Most women, including Latinas, maintained that jobs that paid well and allowed a good quality of life were very important. Schools needed to be decent and safe, and these institutions should make a difference in eradicating many social problems. Reducing the crime rate and violence were other major concerns, as were guns in school and too much sex and violence in the media.

The women maintained that elected officials have made little progress in addressing issues concerning women. Nearly seven out of ten of all women described themselves as "feeling disgusted, frustrated, and disillusioned" with the lack of attention to women's issues. When these women were asked for whom they would vote and what characteristics were important in a political candidate, they responded as follows. First, a very small percentage of women would vote for a candidate based solely on political affiliation; for most women, the candidate's position on issues was more important. The other factors women considered were a candidate's integrity followed by his or her experience. Although a significant majority of women believed that more women should be elected to political office, only one in three would vote for a female candidate based simply on her gender.

The results of these surveys illustrate that Latinas vote on issues, not on party affiliation. They also want to trust their elected officials and feel that they are accountable to the community. Furthermore, Latinas are willing to support both male and female candidates, whereas Latinos are less likely to support female candidates. Social issues, such as school reform, gun control, and local safety are all important issues for Latinas. (See topic

Topic Highlight 6. The Sánchez Sisters

Linda and Loretta Sánchez made history in 2003 as the first sisters ever to win seats in the U.S. Congress at the same time. The Sánchez sisters come from a family of seven children. Born in Lynwood, California, they are the daughters of Mexican immigrants.

Loretta Sánchez was born in 1960. She received her bachelor's degree in economics and master's degree in business from American University. Her congressional district covers Anaheim, Garden Grove, Santa Ana, and Fullerton. She has worked to develop greater economic opportunities for her constituents through enhancing community projects and job creation.

Linda Sánchez was born in 1969. She graduated from Berkeley with a bachelor of arts in Spanish literature with an emphasis on bilingual education. She later received a law degree from the University of California at Los Angeles. Her district covers Artesia, Cerritos, Hawaiian Gardens, Lakewood, Paramount, Southgate, and parts of Whittier and Los Angeles.

Both congresswomen have prioritized policy issues that they believe are important for the growing Latino community, such as crime prevention, education, health care, unemployment, expanded economic opportunities, and job creation. They are members of important committees, including the Judiciary and House Armed Services committees as well as the Select Committee on Homeland Security. They are also members of the Hispanic Caucus and the Women's Caucus and are important players in the Democratic National Committee (Chávez Candelaria, García, and Aldama; United States House of Representatives). ■

highlight 6 for biographies of two Latina congresswomen whose agendas focus on many of these issues.)

■ Feminism and Grassroots Politics

Irrespective of the patterns that discourage Latina participation in **traditional political** outlets, Latinas are not apolitical. On the contrary, women, in comparison to men and regardless of their **ethnicity** or socioeconomic status, are more likely to pursue politics at the local level and for personal reasons, actions that may not be fully recognized. Their activity is also not easily described within the bounds of mainstream **feminism.**

Theoretical feminism, from a political perspective, examines how women organize to counter sexual oppression. The feminism of white mainstream women does not always accurately describe the concerns and activities of Mexican American women, however. Critics note that defining the political actions of Mexican American women simply as a means to end sexual oppression does not take into account the unique cultural and ethnic factors that motivate or hinder their political participation. Furthermore, mainstream feminism does not provide a sufficiently inclusive agenda for Mexican American women. Because the founding members of the feminist movement came from middle-class backgrounds, mainstream feminist platforms do not meet all the needs of Mexican American women, who generally come from poorer backgrounds with strong ties to the Mexican immigrant community (Ruíz and DuBois 2000).

The **Chicano Movement** was important for Mexican American feminism because in many ways it opened the door to greater political participation. More Mexican American women began running for office, whereas others became involved in community-based activist and civic groups, as well as the political campaigns of their spouses. The Chicano Movement not only created a specific political platform around race, gender, and class, it also socialized a large number of Mexican American women to participate in electoral politics. The Chicano Movement also championed several major objectives, such as labor rights and ending segregation, discrimination, and political repression. The fact that **Chicana feminism** was an offshoot of the Chicano Movement is not surprising to historians given that other women of color communities began their feminist organizing activities while participating within larger social and political movements. For instance, Asian American and African American women began organizing within the **Civil Rights Movement.**

During the Chicano Movement, Mexican American women were generally relegated to supporting the needs of the male activists, many of whom professed progressive ideals but operated in the patriarchal style of previous generations (Ruíz and DuBois 2000). In the early days of the movement, and still to some degree today, the issue of male machismo has produced tension between progressive Chicanas and the male-dominated hierarchy of Chicano grassroots and mainstream political organizations (Mirandé and Enríquez 1979). Feeling that Chicana needs were being overlooked, Mexican American women formed their own organizations to mobilize against racial, gender, and cultural oppression. Some Chicanos and Chicanas accused these women of being disloyal to the Chicano Movement, charging that Chicana feminism was akin to selling out to the whites and that their cause divided the Chicano Movement. Similarly, many Chicano males felt that Chicana feminism was a divisive ideology that was incompatible with the Chicano movement (García 2000).

Mexican American women face a multitude of barriers from both American culture at large and their culture of origin. According to the "triple oppression" perspective, the sources of Chicana oppression are threefold: (1) Mexican American women are minorities and confront racism in the United States, (2) Mexican American women must cope with sexism and other barriers related to their gender, and (3) Mexican American women must also contend with oppression at the hands of males in their own community (Riddell 1974). That is to say, husbands, brothers, fathers, and boyfriends may not support women's efforts to participate as equals and may challenge their political participation, especially as leaders. Even today, the overwhelming majority of Hispanic members of Congress are males, many of whom launched their political careers during the Chicano Movement and subsequent grassroots political initiatives (Takash 1993).

■ Community Activism

Politics is not simply about assuming positions. A person usually becomes involved because of their life experiences. I became involved because I saw the lack of educational opportunities in California for Mexican Americans. My parents, who are seventy-one and seventy years old, attended segregated schools and experienced discrimination. My father, Frank, whose first language was Spanish, was hit by his teacher for speaking Spanish in his elementary school class. My mother, Celina, lived close to a school with nice equipment but was not allowed to attend because she was Mexican American. She was bussed to a school farther away from her home. I know that if they had had more positive educational experiences, they would have assumed professional careers. My parents are far more intelligent than I am, but I had better opportunities. I continue to see these inequities play out in the school system today. (Frances M., 36)

Frances illustrates how Latina feminist community activism, or the need to take a stand, is shaped by the importance of family and space for women, a motivation sometimes described as "activist mothering" (Naples 1998). Another common characteristic of women community activists is commitment to community work as part of a larger struggle for social justice. In short, women are committed to change in their community as a way to improve the quality of life for future generations. They feel a sense of promise in changing their communities for the better.

As is true of Latina elected officials, many of these community organizers are influenced by previous work in political organizations. These organizations shape their norms and values as well as set agendas or issues to be undertaken. The culture of the community greatly shapes the agendas women pursue. Some activists pursue agendas within their specific communities whereas others feel a commitment to work on behalf of their people in general, whether or not they live in the same community.

Because many Mexican American women are involved in their church, this can become a meaningful site for political involvement. Religious traditions of social justice and charity toward the poor make the church a strong political influence, a phenomenon called "liberation theology." The church also provides a good forum to disseminate information and take a stand on issues. Furthermore, church members are very familiar with what goes on and the needs that are present in their communities (Cadena and Medina 2004). Many activist women feel they are in a better position than elected officials to mobilize change in their communities. Generally, these women believe that elected officials are motivated by a desire for power not for social change. Therefore, the women feel that they can make a bigger difference at the local level.

■ Chicana Activists

Perhaps the most important study on Mexican American women activists relates to Mothers of East Los Angeles (MELA). These nontraditional political players stopped the building in their community of a 1,700-inmate prison and a waste incinerator that would have been near thirty surrounding schools (Pardo 1997). Pardo concluded that "the women in MELA transformed their traditional networks and resources around family and culture into specific political assets to protect their communities" (Pardo 1997, 151). Because poor people are more likely to live in areas that have environmental risks, environmentalism has become an issue that has successfully mobilized many poorer communities (Prindeville and Bretting 1998).

Many MELA members described their previous political activism as being involved in their children's education or joining parent-school associations, the same background as one of the most famous Chicana activists, Dolores Huerta (see topic highlight 7). Pardo notes that it is in these school organizations that social networks were established. She continues, "They have defied stereotypes of apathy and used ethnic, gender, and class **identity** as an impetus, a strength, a vehicle for political activism. They have expanded their—and our—understanding of the complexities of a political system, and they have reaffirmed the possibility of doing something" (Pardo 1997, 164–65).

■ Binational Activism

Latinos in the United States are more interconnected with Latinos in other Latin American countries than ever before. These **binational** and multinational social and economic relationships are predicted to expand, promoting **pan-ethnicity,** an identity that transcends nation-states. Large multinational companies that operate in both the United States and Latin America, trade policies that encourage bilateral relationships, and immigration that creates international social networks all solidify a bond between U.S. Latinos and Latin Americans.

A growing area of research examines the cooperative organizing strategies of Mexican American women and women in other Latin American countries. In a study focusing on women's organizing at the grassroots level, Nancy Naples (1998) looked at how international investments influence local organizing strategies. She examined a **coalition** called Hermanas en La Lucha/Sisters, a group of women that organized based on Chicana feminism. They linked their struggles with those of the indigenous women of Latin America and Mexico, with whom they share the same needs by

Topic Highlight 7. Dolores C. Huerta

Dolores C. Huerta is the mother of eleven children and a grandmother to fourteen. But she is far better known for helping to give birth to the **United Farm Workers of America,** the union she cofounded with César Chávez. Huerta was born in a mining town in northern New Mexico on April 10, 1930. Her father, Juan Fernandez, was a miner, field worker, union activist, and member of the state assembly. Her parents divorced when she was three. She learned her management skills through watching her mother, Alicia, run a restaurant and seventy-room hotel in Stockton, California.

After a career teaching in the public schools, Huerta left her job because she said she could not stand to see children coming to class hungry and in need of shoes. So she moved on to community activism in 1955. Working for the Community Service Organization, she began to battle segregation and police brutality, to lead voter registration drives, to push for improved public services, and to fight for new legislation.

In 1960, Huerta organized and founded the Agricultural Workers Association. In 1961, she became a lobbyist and successfully pushed to remove citizenship requirements from pension and public assistance programs. Huerta was also instrumental in the passage of legislation that allowed people to vote in Spanish and to take their driver's license tests in their native language. In 1962, she went to Washington, DC, to help end what she described as the "captive labor" Bracero Program. Later that year, the Community Service Organization refused a request from its president, César Chávez, to start organizing farm workers. So Huerta, a single mother of seven children, moved to Delano, California, and helped Chávez form the National Farm Workers Association, which later became the UFW. The pair traveled the California farm country, enlisting members along the way. As a result of a series of boycotts and strikes, the union negotiated labor contracts for tens of thousands of workers, often against stiff opposition by landowners.

In 1963, Huerta helped secure Aid for Dependent Families, which has become a critical assistance program for the unemployed and under-employed. In 1966, Huerta negotiated a collective bargaining contract with the Schenley Wine Company that made history. It was the first contract ever between farmworkers and an agricultural company.

During a strike in 1973, thousands of farmworkers were arrested for picketing, hundreds were beaten, and two were murdered. Despite such dangers, Huerta has continued her work. She has been arrested more than twenty times for her union activities. Her influence in politics also has been substantial. Robert F. Kennedy, moments before he was assassinated, praised Huerta for helping him win the California primary election in 1968. Huerta was inducted in the National Women's Hall of Fame in 1993. She received the American Civil Liberties Union Roger Baldwin Medal of Liberty Award, the Eugene V. Debs Foundation Outstanding American Award, and the Ellis Island Medal of Freedom Award. In 1998, *Ms* magazine chose Huerta as one of its three women of the year. In the same year, the *Ladies Home Journal* included her in its "100 Most Important Women of the 20th Century" (United Farm Workers of America). ■

virtue of colonialism, globalization, race, and gender and class subordination. The Hermanas en La Lucha/Sisters helped generate solidarity on both sides of the U.S.–Mexico border for the Zapatista resistance in Chiapas, Mexico. For example, they initiated the Bread Project, with the proceeds from bread sales going to assist the women of Chiapas. Naples predicts that similar **transnational** organizing groups will continue to flourish.

■ Concluding Thoughts

Chicana feminism has been an important influence in U.S. politics. Many Mexican American women felt that mainstream feminism was important but did not take into account their particular needs. Today, confronting racism and sexism are important political agendas for Mexican American women in both traditional and nontraditional political venues.

The role of women in the political process is multifaceted and complex. Although the number of Mexican American women participating in traditional political outlets is relatively small, recent trends promise growing involvement and influence. A Chicana leader has several characteristics.

She is typically from a working-class background, is educated, and has been politicized through participatory politics at the local level. She usually becomes involved in politics because of a personal commitment to issues that affect her community.

Although it is important to highlight the need for greater Latina involvement in traditional politics, it is just as important to understand the local, participatory, and activist nature of their involvement as distinctive and no less important. As one scholar notes, the political **mobilization** of Latina women is more participatory because they have different perceptions of the nature of politics. Rather than focusing on elected officials, Latinas put their energy toward practical issues related to the community and interpersonal networks (Hardy-Fanta 1993).

There are a growing number of Latina leaders at the local level. The concerns of these women revolve around their community, their space, and their children. Also intriguing is the fact that Mexican American women's identity is being shaped not only by the country in which they reside but also by women in other Latin American countries. This political trend is predicted to continue given the interconnecting forces of immigration, technology, business, and overall pan-ethnicity.

■ **Discussion Exercises**

1. What is Chicana feminism and how is it different from mainstream feminism?

2. What are the typical characteristics of Chicana/Latina elected officials? How are these important in shaping their political activities and agendas?

3. What are some of the issues Mexican American women want politicians to pursue?

4. How do you think politics has transformed women activists at the local, state, and federal levels?

5. What are some of the issues that have mobilized Mexican American women at the grassroots level? Why are these issues of particular importance to Chicanas?

6. What do you predict for the future of women's organizing at the grassroots level?

■ Suggested Readings

Niemann, Yolanda Flores, ed. 2002. *Chicana leadership: The frontiers reader.* Lincoln: University of Nebraska Press.

Pardo, Mary S. 1998. *Mexican American women activists: Identity and resistance in two Los Angeles communities.* Philadelphia: Temple University Press.

Ruíz, Vicki L. 1998. *From out of the shadows: Mexican women in twentieth-century America.* New York: Oxford University Press.

Saldívar-Hull, Sonia. 2000. *Feminism on the border: Chicana gender politics and literature.* Berkeley: University of California Press.

Sierra, Christine Marie, and Adaljisa Sosa-Riddell. 1994. Chicanas as political actors: Rare literature, complex practice. *National Political Science Review* 4: 297–317.

5

Policies and Issues Affecting the
Mexican American Community

The problem with politics is that people are uninformed, especially regarding social issues. Part of the problem of politics is the struggle to
decipher what is true versus what is inaccurate. So much political activity
today thrives on sound bites. The media dictates sound bites, and much of
the American public and political leaders mimic this as a way to convey
messages. (Mathew M., 30)

Anti-immigrant sentiment during the mid- to late 1990s mobilized
the Mexican-origin population in California. In 2000, the largely
immigrant janitorial workforce in Los Angeles successfully organized to improve wages and working conditions. This protest was important because whereas most of the workers were legal immigrants, some
were not, a fact few of their employers were willing to acknowledge
publicly. In 2002, thousands of Mexican Americans in Phoenix, Arizona,
organized to oppose an initiative designed to eradicate bilingual education.
Unfortunately, the proposal passed, but important political networks were
established for future **mobilization.** This chapter highlights some of the
major economic and social trends affecting Mexican Americans and presents some policy recommendations. Two high-level Mexican American
policymakers in the Clinton administration, Henry Cisneros and Bill Richardson, are highlighted in topic highlight 8.

Education

Many Mexican American leaders regard education as the single most critical issue affecting the community. Simply put, the more education an
individual receives, the more opportunities exist to find a good job and
have a high standard of living. Strong correlations also exist between high
social and economic status and the ability to affect political and civic dia-
logue (Verba, Schlozman, and Brady 1995). Tragically, Mexican Ameri-

cans lag behind other U.S. groups in almost every educational measure. Graduation rates among U.S. **Latinos** are among the lowest in the nation, surpassing only those of rural Native Americans in some communities. College and university enrollment, as well as degree attainment rates, are also low.

A key barrier to educational attainment among Mexican-origin schoolchildren is English-language proficiency. Significant numbers of Mexican-origin students are recent immigrants or have been raised in households where Spanish is the dominant language. Meanwhile, anti–bilingual education initiatives across the country have curbed or eliminated many such programs. Approximately 3.5 million U.S. public schoolchildren are limited English proficient, and most of these children are of Latino origin.

Making matters worse, Mexican-origin children face discrimination and other cultural barriers in education. For instance, limited English proficient children are routinely identified by public school systems as developmentally disabled and tracked into special education programs, though these children are very often no less intelligent or capable of learning than their English-proficient peers. In addition, teachers and administrators, who are often not Latino, frequently have low expectations of Mexican-origin schoolchildren and may channel them into less challenging programs (Martínez-Ebers et al. 2000).

Nationally, standardized testing is being used to determine whether students should be advanced or graduated. So-called "underachieving schools"—a designation often arrived at based solely on a school's cumulative standardized test scores—can now be penalized through loss of federal funding. Because Mexican-origin children on average do not perform as well on standardized tests as non-Latino white children, and given that most of these children attend poor, increasingly segregated schools, Mexican-origin students are bound to suffer. They are already a majority of the public school students in certain cities across California, Texas, Arizona, and New Mexico (U.S. Census Bureau 2000b).

Policy Recommendations

- Policies and programs that retain Mexican-origin students in school should be increased and encouraged. Studies illustrate that dropping out of school can be prevented if Mexican-origin middle school students receive support and greater parental involvement.

Topic Highlight 8. Key Latino Policymakers

The following biographies illustrate how greater Mexican American representation in cabinet and policymaking positions can influence policies
that benefit Mexican Americans.

■ Henry Cisneros

Henry Cisneros was born in 1947 in a barrio of San Antonio, Texas. His
roots span more than fifteen generations in the U.S. Southwest. As a
young boy, Henry Cisneros attended parochial schools, which he describes as an important factor in his success. He later went to Texas
Agricultural and Mechanical University, where he earned both bachelor's
and master's degrees in urban planning; later he received his doctorate in
public administration from George Washington University.

His formal political career began as an assistant in the mayor's office in
San Antonio. Cisneros then became the youngest person ever to win a
San Antonio city council position, which he held for two terms. In 1981,
Cisneros was the first Mexican American elected mayor of San Antonio,
a position to which he was reelected three times. Among his accomplish-
ments as mayor, he was responsible for rebuilding the city's economic
base, attracting high-tech industries, increasing tourism, and creating
employment.

In 1992, Henry Cisneros was the first Mexican American appointed to
a federal position, serving as secretary of the Department of Housing
and Urban Development until 1997. After leaving government when his
ongoing payments to a former mistress were disclosed, Cisneros headed
Univision Communications, a multinational Spanish-language media and
television network. He currently runs American City Vista, a real estate
and construction development firm in California (Chávez Candelaria,
García, and Aldama 2004; Kanellos and Pérez 1995).

■ Bill Richardson

Bill Richardson was born in 1947 in Pasadena, California. His mother was a socialite and his father an American banker who raised him in Mexico City. He attended Tufts University for both undergraduate and graduate studies in diplomacy. He unsuccessfully ran for Congress from New Mexico in 1980 but was elected on his second attempt in 1983. A Democrat, Richardson was reelected seven times. He served on several committees, including the House Commerce, Resources, and Intelligence committees, as well as being named Chief Deputy Democratic Whip.

In 1996, he was nominated as the U.S. Permanent Representative to the United Nations. Ambassador Richardson was integral in several diplomatic negotiations, including the freeing of hostages in Croatia, Burma, Cuba, Iraq, North Korea, and Sudan. He also negotiated the peaceful transfer of power in Zaire, among other activities. He has been nominated for the Nobel Peace Prize four times.

In 1998, he was appointed secretary of the U.S. Department of Energy, eventually becoming the highest ranking Latino in the Clinton administration. In 2002, he was elected governor of New Mexico (see figure 12).

■ 12. New Mexico Governor
Bill Richardson

Indicative of the respect New Mexicans have for Governor Richardson, he won by the largest margin since the 1962 election. ■

- Mexican-origin students complain that their school curriculum is not relevant to their lives. It would be a positive and motivating change to have historical figures and literature that mirror their cultural experiences integrated into course work. Studies illustrate that being able to relate to the curriculum encourages greater educational participation.

- Politicians advocate for more standardized testing as a way to improve school achievement. However, these exams do not always accurately assess the talents or needs of students, particularly Mexican immigrant or first-generation Mexican American students. Standardized testing should be discouraged as a significant means of assessing student achievement. It should be used as a tool to indicate areas of weakness that perhaps disproportionately affect Mexican-origin students, but not as the main indicator of performance. Undoubtedly, there are problems in the U.S. public education system, but it is naïve to assume that blanket standardized tests are the solution.

- Most minority students will not attend college because they cannot afford to do so. Furthermore, Mexican immigrant students may be deterred from going to college if they are charged out-of-state tuition or denied entrance because of their immigrant status. Bills have been proposed in Congress to deny undocumented immigrants access to universities. More scholarships or tuition remissions are needed in order to increase admission and retention of Mexican-origin students.

- Recent elections in California and Arizona have all but eradicated bilingual education in those states. Opponents of bilingual education maintain that the programs are not effective and keep students at a disadvantage because they learn English more slowly. Advocates of bilingual education maintain that Latino students need such programs to improve their educational access and that learning in both English and Spanish encourages better learning overall. Bilingual education should not be eradicated but rather improved. Better approaches to teaching students in both languages would better prepare them to communicate and compete in a global economy and an increasingly bilingual U.S. culture.

- Certified, qualified teachers should continue to teach bilingual education and English as a second language courses. Bilingual education should not be eradicated on a state-by-state basis. Rather school districts should provide several alternatives to students who need assistance, allowing parents a more proactive role in their children's learning.

■ Community

The communities where people of Mexican origin live raise important considerations for policymakers. A good community is characterized by abundant jobs, a sufficient tax base to generate adequate public services for its citizens, and fair political representation. A community that has significant numbers of low-income residents must allocate many of its valuable resources to providing fire, police, health, and social services but may not receive sufficient funds to subsidize these costs (Peterson 1981). Most important, if the community lacks adequate services, people are less likely to invest in it.

Manufacturing jobs formerly located predominantly in urban areas are leaving North America for Asian or Latin American countries. The loss of jobs hurts not only Mexican Americans but also the surrounding communities. When companies leave, areas are devastated through widespread unemployment. Sectors that served the needs of businesses are also affected. Future economic investment in these areas is unlikely and cities are hard-pressed to find replacement businesses.

The U.S. economy is increasingly dependent on highly skilled, technologically savvy workers. Mexican Americans must be prepared to participate in this economy, or there will be a further decline in their income relative to other groups and they are likely to be increasingly concentrated in the service sector in jobs that lack benefits.

Many analysts predict continued outmigration from cities to the suburbs. This means that those who live in the suburbs are likely to be better represented politically than those who remain in the core urban areas. Elected officials, such as city council members, are able to mobilize suburban voters around homeownership and school taxation issues. Those who live in urban areas need effective political representation but they will be the least likely to receive it.

Policy Recommendations

■ Unfortunately, service sector employees are primarily of Mexican origin. The minimum wage should be increased in order to improve the quality of life and living conditions of these workers.

- The Occupational Safety and Health Administration (OSHA) should monitor worksites that hire mostly Mexican-origin workers to ensure that these workers are treated fairly and have safe working conditions. Unfortunately, small firms, which are likely to hire Mexican immigrants, are difficult to monitor.

■ Feeling of Connection

Mexican Americans' views on crime are shaped by their experiences and by law enforcement agencies, such as the police and the **INS** (Magaña 1999). Studies indicate that increased Mexican American representation in public agencies improves the treatment of clients who are from similar backgrounds. Street-level officials and service providers have the most influence over policy decisions and how individuals view their government (Lipsky 1980). Police, teachers, social workers, and city workers all fall into this category.

Furthermore, people of Mexican origin participate in their communities in unique ways. Two of the best examples are how they participate in organized sports and in their church. Sporting events provide opportunities for players and families to get together and strengthen the informal social networks through which they obtain vital information about daily life, such as city services, transportation, and cultural events (Menjívar and Magaña 2002). They are also active in a variety of religious communities, filling the pews at Catholic parishes, and increasingly at mainline Protestant churches and smaller evangelical churches. The church has always occupied a prominent place in the lives of people of Mexican origin in the United States through its sponsorship of an intricate welfare system to serve the needs of the community. These spaces also provide opportunities to build and maintain important social networks with friends, neighbors, and others from their countries (Menjívar and Magaña 2002).

Policy Recommendations

- Many cities with large Mexican-origin populations are seeking to recruit and retain more Mexican American civil servants in service delivery positions. Research illustrates that when civil servants mirror the **demographic** makeup of their community, they can more actively represent its needs. Therefore, cities with large Mexican-origin populations should hire more Mexican American teachers, police officers, social workers, and other service providers.

- Monies allocated, either private or public, to support cultural events through churches or sports teams would further promote a positive sense of community. Too often, cultural, artistic, and community events are eradicated or poorly funded.

- Supporting local activities such as celebrations of key holidays that mirror the culture of the community would be another important policy. Simply put, city leaders need to encourage a greater sense of community in Mexican-origin neighborhoods. The benefits of this type outreach are various and include reducing crime and improving safety.

■ Immigration

Mexicans make up the largest legal and illegal immigrant group in the United States. Mexicans have migrated to the United States for a myriad of reasons including unsafe living conditions and lack of employment opportunities in Mexico, as well as ongoing demand for cheap labor in the United States. Immigration is also the result of economic expansion policies implemented by both the United States and Mexico.

Figures for undocumented immigrants are never precise. Nevertheless, the best estimates put the overall undocumented immigrant population at somewhere around 3 percent of the total U.S. population, with approximately half of that population coming from Mexico. Furthermore, almost half of undocumented immigrants are people who entered the United States legally for business or pleasure then failed to leave when their visas expired.

Unskilled immigrants continue to meet U.S. demands for cheap labor. Studies indicate that American citizens tend to avoid certain jobs, such as those in the service sector, and that using immigrant labor keeps prices lower. Therefore, immigrants will continue to fill labor needs in both the agricultural and service sectors.

In the 1990s, immigration reforms focused on increased border surveillance. There was a 300 percent increase in the funding for the policing of immigrants, particularly in southern border states such as Texas and California. The tighter patrols in these areas have led to more immigrants attempting to cross the border in remote areas, particularly in Arizona.

Summer temperatures in the Nogales, Arizona, region can reach a staggering 120 degrees. Unfortunately, immigrants unprepared for the brutal Arizona climate may not be found before they succumb to heat exposure because there are relatively few border patrol agents in the area. The result has been an alarming rise in the number of immigrant deaths in the desert, which have virtually quadrupled since 1993.

Several initiatives have been passed to deny public services to Latino immigrants. In 1994 California passed perhaps the most controversial proposition, **Proposition 187,** dubbed the "Save Our State Initiative." It required school and university administrators to verify the citizenship status of all newly admitted students as well as their parents. Students and parents unable to prove their legal right to live in the United States were to be deported. This initiative also prohibited all hospitals, both public and private, from providing nonemergency health care to undocumented immigrants. Proposition 187 was eventually found to be unconstitutional.

Policy Recommendations

Policies that would take into account the growing and ever-present immigrant population include the following:

- The role of the INS in the lives of Mexican immigrants should be considered in immigration debates as well as policy reform.

- Funding should be redirected from the enforcement of immigration laws to serving the needs of legal immigrants and ensuring that the civil rights of U.S. citizens of Mexican origin are not violated by the INS.

- U.S. President George Bush and Mexican President Vicente Fox are considering another temporary worker program or **Bracero-type program.** This **binational** program would allow Mexican laborers to enter the country legally on a seasonal basis. The program has the support of several governors from southwestern states as a more humane approach to curbing illegal immigration. Provided that better safeguards are in place to prevent the widespread worker abuses of the previous Bracero Program, policymakers should strongly support this proposal.

- Policymakers are also considering another **amnesty** program that would legalize the status of undocumented immigrants who have lived in the United States since 1986. Estimates put the number of immigrants eligible for amnesty at around three million. The political potential of this proposal is that three million Mexican Americans can eventually gain citizenship and be eligible to vote. Since the September 11 attacks, immigration reform for Mexican undocumented immigrants has been put on hold to deal with other issues, such as national security and the war in Iraq. Mexican American **constituents** should strongly voice support for another amnesty.

- Up until the 1950s, job skills were not a major consideration in the admission of immigrants to this country because immigrants were easily absorbed into jobs that did not require much training. Today, this simply is not the case. As evidence, Microsoft owner Bill Gates recently testified to Congress that he desperately needed workers for his company and argued that visa restrictions placed on highly skilled workers should be eased in order to fill labor needs. The service sector is also in need of low-skilled employees. Clearly, both high-skilled and low-skilled immigrant workers are important for the U.S. economy. Congress should push to allow legal immigration of both high- and low-skilled workers from Mexico, in order to meet employment needs in the United States.

■ Health and Safety

Mexican-origin families continue to face a multitude of health and safety problems because of where they live and their types of employment. Because they generally have low levels of education, Mexican-origin workers tend to be employed in jobs that are hazardous or in conditions that are unsafe. Because some of them work in seasonal or temporary labor or as part of the **informal economy,** federal safety standards are often not enforced and, needless to say, these jobs do not provide insurance or benefits. Furthermore, people of Mexican origin tend to live in poor urban areas, which tend to be unsafe and have more environmental hazards, such as toxic waste sites.

Private health-care insurance is expensive and beyond the financial reach of many Mexican American and immigrant families. Studies indicate that people of Mexican origin who lack insurance tend not to seek medical assistance until they are very sick because they cannot afford to pay medical expenses out of pocket. As a result, diseases that could have been managed or cured if detected early are not identified until they require major medical intervention or are even beyond treatment. Another consequence of the high uninsured rate is that many use patchwork helpers such as urgent care centers or emergency rooms (de la Torre and Estrada 2001).

Culture and gender both play important roles in Mexican Americans' access to health care. Researchers note that people of Mexican origin are less likely than other people to go to the doctor because it is not culturally acceptable to get sick (de la Torre and Estrada 2001). Thus, women may not seek preventive health care, such as pap smears and mammograms. Furthermore, HIV disease (the virus that causes AIDS) is rising in the Mexican American female population. Mexican American males are more likely than average to suffer from chronic illnesses such as diabetes, cardiovascular problems, cancer, and high cholesterol. Many of these diseases are preventable and linked to poor diet and exercise.

Mexican-origin children are less likely than most to be immunized and are more likely to be obese and develop diet-related diabetes. Because many of these children live in unsafe areas, they are also less likely to exercise, compounding the dietary risks. Poverty is also linked to adolescent diabetes, early sexual activity, and teen pregnancy (de la Torre and Estrada 2001). In sum, where Mexican-origin people live, the kind of work they perform, and their cultural views regarding health issues are all inextricably related to a pattern of poor health care.

Policy Recommendations

Enacting policies that focus on preventive health care would be an important start for policymakers seeking to meet the needs of the Mexican-origin community.

- Free proactive medical assistance and health outreach, such as checkups and immunizations, should be made more available. Unfortunately, significantly cutting or denying indigent health services is often advocated as a way to generate monies for the state. For instance, Californians overwhelmingly passed Proposition 187, an initiative that would have essentially eradicated these types of social services for undocumented immigrants had it not been overturned in court, and a similar proposal is being considered by voters in Arizona. In the long run, implementing preventive health care costs less than providing emergency care once a medical condition becomes critical. For instance, the cost of educating people on the dangers of diabetes and providing support with lifestyle changes is far less than the medical treatment for advanced diabetes.

- Preventive health care, such as free screening and immunizations, is often cut as ways to decrease spending. Furthermore, approaches to dealing with social problems are often overlooked because politicians want quick solutions. This means that groups who are affected by social and economic reforms must be proactive and demand greater access to social and health services.

■ Mexican American and Immigrant Employment

The data illustrate that people of Mexican origin are valuable consumers in today's economy. Because the population is one of the fastest growing in the nation and is demographically younger, they have substantial purchasing power. The economic effects of Mexican immigrants as consumers have also been researched and may be surprising to the general public. An accurate assessment of the net costs and benefits of immigration is very difficult, partly because of the size of the population and partly because many immigrants remain hidden for fear of deportation. Yet studies consistently indicate that the presence of Mexican immigrants in the economy results in a net gain in federal and local tax revenue, as well as overall spending on goods and services. Their presence also creates jobs for American workers and does not appear to have a significant effect in displacing American workers from jobs nor in lowering wages (Briggs and Moore 1994).

Small businesses, those employing fewer than fifty employees, are more likely than large firms to hire Mexican immigrants. These companies usually attract employees through social networks rather than paid advertising. Undocumented workers are susceptible to wage and employment exploitation. They are deported and repatriated in times of high unemployment, and they may be scapegoated for social problems. Immigration laws such as employer sanctions may also result in employment discrimination, whereby employers may be reluctant to hire Mexican Americans or legal Mexican immigrants for fear that their documentation may be falsified (Cornelius 1998).

There is also a growing relationship between people of Mexican-origin and union organizing. In the past, unions typically did not want to become involved with Mexican Americans, and particularly Mexican immigrants, because it was believed that they took American jobs. Recently unions have moved away from this belief and begun openly recruiting immigrants. On May 6, 2001, the *San Diego Union-Tribune* reported,

> Under Sweeney, with prodding from the grass roots in places like Los Angeles, the AFL-CIO dramatically reversed its traditional position on immigrants, seeing them as potential allies to be organized rather than threats to American workers. By a fortuitous convergence, labor's shift to a pro-immigrant stance coincided with the reign of California Gov. Pete Wilson, whose flagrantly anti-immigrant position has wrecked the Republican Party's hopes with **Hispanics** in California for at least a generation. . . . Though the national media has not paid much attention, local living wage campaigns, built on local organizing, have succeeded in city after city. . . . Just when grass-roots politics looks moribund, it revives in unexpected places. (Kuttner 2001)

Immigrants are highly entrepreneurial. The businesses of immigrants, however, may not be assessed as part of the formal economy so their actions may be underestimated. Immigrant businesses are not fully accepted by communities nor seen as positive attributes. For instance, street vendors have been the target of reform in many large immigrant communities. Some officials think these businesses should be regulated whereas others think they should be ignored.

Policy Recommendations

- Programs that encourage Mexican American–owned businesses should be supported at the local level. Many small businesses fail because they cannot compete with larger more established companies.

- Unions should be encouraged to continue their outreach to Mexican Americans and Mexican immigrants. Because immigrants are highly entrepreneurial as well as important laborers for the American economy, it is highly desirable to have a strong voice on their behalf in order to serve their needs.

Federal Interventions

Whereas poverty rates have decreased in parts of the country, they have not in Mexican-origin communities. For instance, the number of people living in high-poverty neighborhoods rose 26 percent in California, where people of Mexican origin predominantly reside. Furthermore, 2000 census data illustrate that the new employment generated was mostly in low-paying service jobs (U.S. Census Bureau 2000b). The following account illustrates the challenges these people face:

> In San Diego County, many residents of poor neighborhoods are living on the low wages they earn in the service sector. "After we pay rent we have very little left. We come to the church to ask for food," said Magdaleno Villegas, 46, a restaurant worker whose family of nine has lived in several of San Diego's poorest neighborhoods. He pays $1,300 a month for a four-bedroom apartment in a poor section of Linda Vista. His oldest son, 21-year-old Ismael, is holding two restaurant jobs that pay $8 an hour to support the family while Villegas heals from a work injury. (Sánchez 2003)

The federal government has taken various approaches to addressing the needs of the poor. Perhaps the most proactive stand was taken during Great Depression of the 1930s and into the 1940s, when unemployment compensation, the Civilian Conservation Corps, work relief programs, credit and loans programs, public work projects, federal housing assistance, youth associations, and the Social Security Act were introduced. In the 1960s **War on Poverty,** the Johnson administration implemented similar government interventions. These programs were successful in stimulating the economy as well as assisting the poor.

In the 1980s, new approaches to local and state intervention came into play. Critics of these approaches to poverty felt that the government took too strong a role in state and local affairs and that federal programs developed to help the poor created a society that was overly reliant on government assistance. Others felt the government was too large and should be streamlined. As a result, many social service programs were either drastically downsized or eradicated. For instance, under the Reagan administration there were decreases in public service employment, subsidized housing, work incentive programs, training and employment services, and low-income assistance. Recent decisions by the Bush administration follow along the same lines of reducing government spending on the poor (Morales and Bonilla 1993).

Policy Recommendations

- Given the growing size of the Mexican American community, it is important to maintain policies and programs that address the mobility, economic status, and age of the population. Such programs should be expanded rather than cut.

- Politicians should meaningfully debate and consider these programs and policies as solutions to issues. Too many politicians have been elected on platforms of cutting social services.

■ Concluding Thoughts

This chapter has explored some of the issues and public policies that are most important to the Mexican-origin community. It is important to highlight once again that politics is not just about voting or having electoral representation. To think about politics without knowing where and how people live would be nearsighted. Political behavior should not be measured simply by **voter turnout** but by a variety of factors, such as education, economic mobility, immigration status, and government intervention, to name but a few. I predict a greater political focus on these issues will spawn **grassroots** mobilization strategies.

■ Discussion Exercises

1. What are some policy recommendations for improving the quality of life for Mexican Americans and Mexican immigrants?

2. Why do you think some policies and programs designed to help Mexican Americans have failed? Give examples.

3. What are some of the misconceptions about public policies and their effect on the Mexican-origin community?

4. Based on demographic projections, what are your predictions for the future of Mexican-origin communities? How can problems in the communities be addressed?

■ Suggested Readings

Olivas, Louis. 2002. *Arizona Hispanics: The evolution of influence.* 81st Arizona Town Hall. Tempe: Arizona State University.

Pastor, Manuel. 1993. Latinos and the Los Angeles uprising: The economic context. Report. Los Angeles, CA: Tomás Rivera Policy Institute.

Pulido, Laura. 1996. *Environmentalism and economic justice: Two Chicano struggles in the Southwest.* Tucson: University of Arizona Press.

Rodríguez, David. 2002. *Latino national political coalitions: Struggles and challenges.* New York: Routledge.

Saito, Leland T. 1998. *Race and politics: Asian Americans, Latinos, and Whites in a Los Angeles suburb.* Urbana: University of Illinois Press.

Torres, Rodolfo D., and George Katsiaficas. 1999. *Latino social movements, historical and theoretical perspectives: A new political science reader.* New York: Routledge.

6

Implications for the Future

In some ways Mexican American political leaders have a free ride. Their constituencies are not as demanding as the constituencies of other politicians, but the Mexican American population is growing and maturing. There will be greater power. Immigration reform laws and the adverse impact on Mexican immigrants made many realize the importance of becoming citizens and participating in politics so that they get the available services of the society. (Miguel M., 61)

Demographic projections indicate that the overall size of the Mexican-origin population will continue to escalate, largely due to immigration. Furthermore, as Mexican American children grow up, the potential number of eligible voters increases. The sheer growth of this group will not necessarily equate into more political participation, however. Political leaders need to mobilize Mexican Americans and consider the unique dynamics that define this population. This chapter provides recommendations for mobilizing the Mexican American community.

■ Immigration Issues

If current trends continue, the influence of Mexican-origin immigrants on politics may be substantial in the coming decades. In 2000, there were an estimated 7.8 million foreign-born immigrants living in the United States. **Latinos,** mostly of Mexican origin, make up roughly half of this population. According to the 2000 U.S. Census, 88 percent of the foreign born who identified Latin America as their region of origin were eighteen years or older, but only 28 percent were naturalized citizens. Among Mexican-origin respondents, 38 percent were naturalized citizens. These figures may well underrepresent the untold millions of undocumented immigrants who settle in the United States or cyclically migrate to and from Mexico, as well as the thousands of Mexican immigrants who enter legally but are awaiting legal disposition by the **INS.**

Increased **naturalization** rates would add to the total number of actual and potential voters. Research finds that recently naturalized citizens are active voters (NALEO 1989). Encouraging naturalization entails teaching immigrants about the importance of citizenship, as well as helping them through the complicated process of naturalization. NALEO conducts workshops in Latino communities that have been very successful in reaching the immigrant population. Assistance with processing naturalization paperwork and practicing interview questions in preparation for interacting with U.S. immigration authorities are other valuable methods for increasing voters.

Critics have charged that the naturalization process is too inconsistent, backlogged, and nonsystematic. For instance, some immigrants complain about the random nature of the citizenship interview exams and that they are unable to pass them. Another criticism is that the INS is overwhelmed because agents must process a growing number of immigrants, with the result that the process takes longer than it should. New procedures to speed up the naturalization process should be instituted.

Unfortunately, the numbers of **Hispanics** who are becoming naturalized has decreased over the last four decades. For instance, 75 percent of Hispanics who entered the United States before 1970 became naturalized citizens. For those who entered between 1980 and 1989, the percentage dropped to 24 percent. More recent figures indicate another dramatic decrease in naturalizations. Only 7 percent of the total Hispanic population that entered the country between 1990 and 2000 became citizens (U.S. Census Bureau 2000a). Yet Mexican-origin immigrants make up the largest group applying for admission into the United States and for naturalization. Figures 13–15 show that Mexicans are the largest group applying for citizenship as well as the regions of the country where naturalization outreach should be targeted.

All told, at least twice as many people immigrate to the United States from Mexico than from other Latin American countries. Ultimately, proposed reforms to immigration, in particular proposals to offer a blanket **amnesty,** potentially to millions of illegal immigrants, could further expand the ranks of Mexican American voters. Amnesty was previously offered in 1986 under the **Immigration Reform and Control Act** (IRCA), legalizing millions of undocumented immigrants in the United States, many of whom are today voting **constituents.**

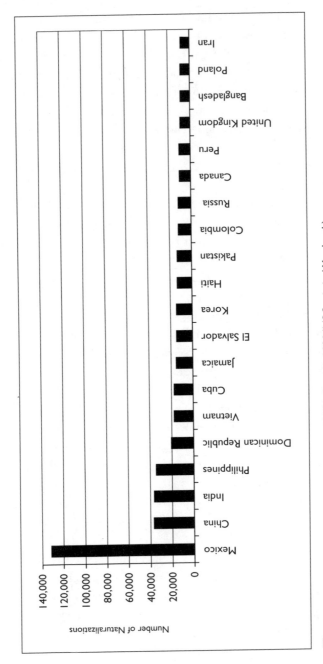

13. Immigrants admitted by country of origin, 1996 (Source: 1998 INS Statistical Yearbook)

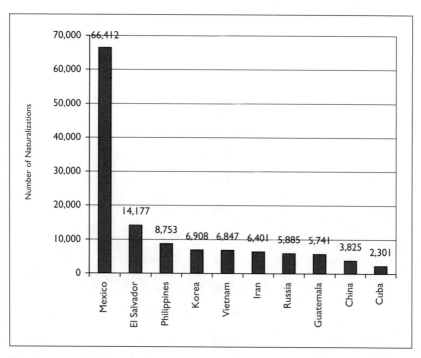

■ 14. Naturalized citizens by country of origin, 1996 (Source: 1998 INS Statistical Year-book)

■ Coalitions

Mexican Americans have essential political resources, such as the size of the population, their cohesiveness, and their intensity, that make them important players in **coalitions.** Historians have noted, however, that Mexican American political elites have been unwilling in the past to align themselves with more powerful groups. Leaders of the **Chicano Movement,** for example, did not advocate working with groups that were involved in partisan politics, for fear that their agendas would be placed aside in order to accommodate more mainstream issues.

Coalitions with African American or women's groups and unions, for instance, could be very effective in garnering support for **affirmative action;** a cleaner, safer environment; good housing; improved education; and less crime; to name but a few issues. Increasing the minimum wage is another initiative that transcends race, gender, and **ethnicity.**

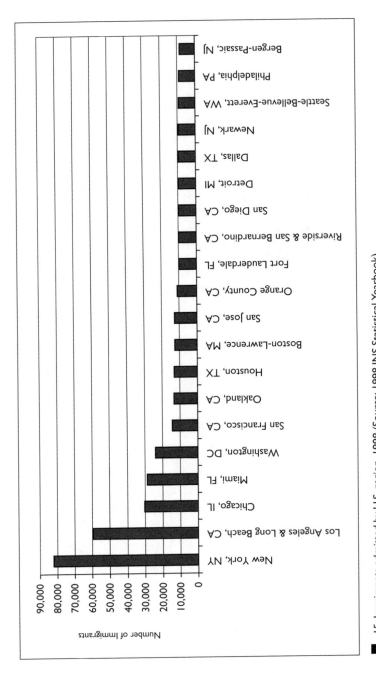

15. Immigrants admitted by U.S. region, 1998 (Source: 1998 INS Statistical Yearbook)

As Mexican American political clout grows, coalition building becomes increasingly important. But coalitions should be based on common interests not primarily on gender, ethnic, or racial considerations. In the U.S. Congress, the Hispanic Caucus has been most effective when it has joined forces with other interest groups, such as the Congressional Black Caucus.

■ Grassroots Politics

Mobilizing Mexican Americans at the local level has proved successful. Creating agendas that are relevant and meaningful has gotten first-time players involved in politics. Many Mexican American elected officials began their political careers at the **grassroots** level. Therefore, training and workshops for leaders at the local level should be encouraged.

The research on grassroots organizing suggests that women are particularly active at this level and should be encouraged and prepared for leadership roles. Furthermore, grassroots organizing is no longer limited to issues within one's community, or even one's country. As communities continue to connect to others outside the United States, international influence at the local level will continue to be important.

■ Political Organizations

Political organizations should also work harder to represent the Mexican-origin community. For those unable to vote, political organizations have the power to influence key decisions on their behalf. Whereas 52 percent of all whites belong to some political organization, only 27 percent of Latino citizens do (García and de la Garza 1985). Among Latino subgroups, the Latino National Political Survey found that voters of Puerto Rican or Mexican origin are less likely to be involved in political organizations than are Cuban Americans. That said, Mexican Americans who can voice their opinion must make sure the organizations they join do not neglect the needs of the voiceless. Organizations should also be prepared to deal with issues that are **binational** in focus. Growing concern for Mexicans living in the United States has resulted in the establishment of important political and **lobbying** groups for the growing immigrant community.

▮ Evolving Political Identity

Identity remains an important consideration in political **mobilization,** and Mexican Americans can no longer be defined monolithically. Census data indicate that race and ethnic identities have evolved over the last few decades. Individuals may define themselves using multiple identifiers, such as Hispanic and African American.

Furthermore, the intermarriage rate among Mexican Americans is also increasing. In part this phenomenon is attributed to more women working outside the home, as well as to migration into locations that are not predominantly Mexican American. Whereas almost half of all Mexican Americans marry other Mexican Americans, the remaining half marry Anglos, African Americans, and people of other ethnicities. As a result, the identity of Mexican Americans will continue to evolve.

Immigration continues to influence identity as well. The second largest "Mexican" city is Los Angeles. Latino identity continues to be shaped by the fact that large portions of the population are native to different countries. This molds not only identity but also how political players view Latinos, frame agendas, and create public policy.

As technology improves and media outlets become more accessible, the physical border between the United States and Mexico holds less importance. Individuals can now access cultural resources from either country without physically entering it. Researchers contend that the ability to enter other spaces without leaving your home has a profound influence on identity (Torres and Katsiaficas 1999).

The flow of labor and production between the United States and Mexico is expected to continue. In southwestern states, for instance, the back-and-forth phenomenon of laborers working in the United States and living in Mexico is common. The phenomena of dual identity and citizenship should be strongly considered by political pundits who are courting this group.

Mexican Americans no longer reside predominantly in the U.S. Southwest. Mexican American populations are expected to continue growing in regions all over the United States, meeting growing employment needs in the Midwest and the South. This is important because where one lives influences one's views issues and what agendas are politically relevant.

■ Religion

Mexican Americans overwhelmingly define themselves as Catholic. Recent surveys indicate that almost 80 percent of the group affiliates with the Catholic religion or are practicing members (Cadena and Medina 2004). First-generation Mexican Americans are more likely to be practicing Catholics than are subsequent generations. Catholic churches can be important spaces for disseminating information as well as liberating and mobilizing communities for change. Furthermore, church leaders are familiar with locally relevant issues. Research on grassroots politics illustrates that local-level strategies coordinated through the church have been very successful for the Mexican-origin community. Protestant and Pentecostal denominations are also making inroads into the Mexican-origin community. These other denominations provide social networks and support for newly arrived immigrants and may provide other avenues for political mobilization.

■ Electoral Politics

The overall growth of the population will continue to fuel their representation in **traditional politics,** through, for example, more elected officials and greater **voter turnout** for initiatives, reforms, and political candidates. Just like the community itself, Mexican American politics will remain diverse.

Research must further investigate the changing needs and demographics of the Mexican American community. One important question is how gender affects political outcomes. Women are playing key roles in politics but very few studies have addressed their participation. Binational influences, such as the influence of the United States on the Mexican community, is another important area of exploration (Darder and Torres 1998). As evidence, remittances, monies sent to families in Mexico from individuals living in the United States, represent a major economic contribution to the Mexican economy. Research on the role of first-generation Mexican Americans in political mobilization strategies should also be developed. Because half of the Mexican American population is foreign born, research as to how to incorporate these individuals is imperative.

Other strategies to encourage greater electoral participation include promoting and developing accessible voter registration procedures. Studies show that, compared to other racial and ethnic groups, a greater percentage of Mexican American voters turn out to vote. They must hold their elected officials accountable as well as contact elected representatives at all levels in order to voice their concerns. If Mexican American voter turnout is substantial, elected officials will represent them more effectively.

Local Mexican American elected officials should be encouraged to run for higher-level offices, say at the state or national level. Research indicates that many elected officials started in local elected positions or at the grassroots level in nontraditional political outlets.

Ultimately, voting must be accessible. In the days before the passage of the **VRA,** overt racism blocked many Mexican Americans, as well as other minorities, from exercising their right to vote. Some argue that to a lesser degree such barriers still exist, though they are more subtle. For instance, Democratic Latino legislators in Arizona in 2003 argued that a **conservative** Republican proposal to require photo identification to cast a ballot was aimed primarily at discouraging Mexican American voter participation, especially since the overwhelming majority of these voters tend to vote for Democratic candidates.

Political parties have paid increasing attention to the potential voting power of Mexican Americans. In Texas, California, and Florida, these voters can mean the difference between winning or losing an election. Political parties must make sure their candidates will represent Mexican American interests.

The Democratic Party cannot take Mexican Americans for granted, even though most align themselves with that party. In states like Texas where there is a strong Republican influence, some Mexican Americans have switched their party affiliation. Political parties have to conduct further outreach in the Mexican American community, including running political commercials in Spanish. The Democratic and Republican parties must also develop agendas that meet the needs of the Mexican American community.

The Republican Party learned that an anti-immigrant position will cause backlash from the Latino community. The party is still trying to counter attacks that it is anti-Latino. Republican positions championing immigration reforms and repealing affirmative action have not gone over well in the community. More recent pro-Latino, nonpartisan approaches have included immigrant worker programs, amnesty, labor reforms, and economic stimulation approaches.

■ Concluding Thoughts

Given that the Mexican-origin population continues to grow in numbers, and that a large part of this growth is attributable to immigration, their political activity will continue to take place in traditional and nontraditional settings. While increasing the number of registered Mexican American voters and elected officials are important steps, it is also essential to acknowledge and encourage the grassroots activities of individuals involved in political mobilization and policy agenda setting. Both approaches to politics are part of the Mexican American political experience.

■ GLOSSARY

affirmative action: Government policies developed to increase minorities' and women's access to job and educational opportunities.

amnesty: A pardon granted to a group of individuals, specifically a provision in the Immigration Reform and Control Act of 1986 that allowed immigrants living illegally in the United States legal resident status if they could prove continuous residence for at least four years.

at-large voting: In a local election, a regulation allowing all eligible voters to vote for all candidates, even those who don't directly represent them. This generally makes it more difficult for minority candidates or those who represent the views of a particular constituency to be elected. *See also* district voting.

binational: Of or belonging to two countries; in the context of this book, Mexico and the United States.

Bracero Program: A binational guest worker program set up between the United States and Mexico to fill employment needs, mostly agricultural, in the United States.

Chicana feminism: A movement that mobilized Mexican American women to empower themselves against sexual, race, and cultural oppression.

Chicano: A term for Americans of Mexican descent. The term often connotes political activism on the behalf of Mexican Americans.

Chicano Movement: A political movement of the 1960s and 1970s in which Mexican Americans sought political empowerment and equal rights as U.S. citizens.

Civil Rights Movement: A movement of the 1960s that sought to end the historic discrimination against African Americans and guarantee them their rights under the U.S. constitution, including freedom of expression, voting rights, equal education, and fair access to opportunities afforded to Anglos.

class: A group of people sharing a similar level of wealth.

coalition: An alliance of several groups with similar interests who work together in order to accomplish a goal.

conservatism: A political ideology that prefers the previous or existing state of affairs. It often opposes efforts to bring about sharp changes in society. *See also* liberalism.

constituents: Individuals who are able to elect a particular political representative; this would include U.S. citizens over eighteen years of age who are registered to vote and reside in that politician's district.

demographics: Descriptive data or information used to project and describe individual and social behavior, including age, types of employment, socioeconomic status, and language use.

district voting: A process used in local elections in which only voters in a particular district can vote for the representative of that district. This facilitates the election of candidates that represent the particular interests of the constituents of each individual district; for example, the election of a minority candidate to represent a district with a large minority population. *See also* at-large voting.

ethnicity: Identification with a particular group that has distinct racial, linguistic, or religious features.

feminism: A movement that seeks to end gender discrimination and grant women equal political, social, and economic opportunities.

gerrymandering: Setting the boundaries of electoral districts to favor one political party and concentrate the opposition in as few districts as possible.

grassroots politics: Political mobilization that is locally based around issues relevant and specific to the community.

Great Society programs: An initiative of the Lyndon Johnson Administration that sought to eliminate poverty and improve the environment and educational system.

Hispanic: A term for people of Latin American descent who live in the United States. *See also* Latino.

identity: How a person defines himself or herself based on factors such as race, class, gender, sexual preference, or political affiliation. One's identity has a strong influence on how one views political issues.

Immigration Act of 1965: An act of Congress that lifted the numerical quotas on immigrant groups that had been established in the early twentieth century. More important, the act set up a family preference system whereby immigrants living legally in the United States could sponsor family members to enter the United States, thus significantly facilitating their migration into the country.

Immigration and Naturalization Service (INS): The federal agency responsible for the enforcement of immigration law and conferring U.S. citizenship on immigrants.

Immigration Reform and Control Act (IRCA): An act passed in 1986 designed to control illegal immigration through two provisions, amnesty and employer sanctions. Amnesty granted legal resident status to immigrants who entered the United States illegally if they could prove that they had worked and lived in the country continuously and had no criminal convictions. Employer sanctions punish employers who knowingly hired undocumented workers.

informal economy: Labor and economic contributions that are not captured by formal measures of economic activity, including the activities of undocumented workers.

La Raza Unida Party (LRU): A short-lived political party founded to meet the specific needs of Mexican Americans and arising out of the Chicano Movement. The political party was successful in running candidates at the local level of government in states such as Texas, California, and Colorado.

Latino: A term used to describe U.S. residents who were born in or whose ancestors come from Latin American countries, including Mexico, Central and South America, Puerto Rico, and Cuba. Some prefer this term to Hispanic. *See also* Hispanic.

liberalism: A political ideology that advocates the use of government resources for social programs to assist those less fortunate and that is associated with tolerance for all groups, regardless of ethnicity, race, gender, and sexual orientation.

lobbying groups: Also called interest groups or pressure groups, these groups advocate or oppose certain issues. Lobby groups have been formed to support the rights and privileges of Mexican immigrants and Mexican Americans.

mobilization: Political outreach by political party representatives, elected officials, or grassroots organizers to recruit participants in their causes.

naturalization: The process of conferring U.S. citizenship on a person who was born in a foreign country.

naturalized: Describes a person who has been through the process of naturalization.

New Deal: Government programs and policies of the Franklin Roosevelt administration designed to ease poverty and unemployment during the Great Depression.

nontraditional politics: Political mobilization strategies that include grassroots efforts, informal political organizations, and local entities such as churches.

Paisano Program: Also known as the **Compatriot Program,** policies designed to ease travel restrictions between the United States and Mexico.

pan-ethnicity: An identity that encompasses all ethnic groups as opposed to being restricted to one's country of origin.

Proposition 187:   A ballot initiative also known as the "Save Our State Initiative" passed in California in 1994. It denied education and most publicly funded services, unless on an emergency basis, to undocumented immigrants. This proposition was ruled unconstitutional in a court challenge.

traditional politics: Political mobilization strategies that include representation by elected officials, turning out to vote for ballot issues and candidates, and political parties' attempts to represent constituents' needs.

transnational: The interconnection of countries through such venues as multinational companies, immigration, and technology.

United Farm Workers of America (UFW):   A union founded by civil rights activists César Chávez and Dolores Huerta in the early 1960s to protect migrant farmworkers from labor abuses and unsafe working conditions.

voter turnout: The number of voters who cast ballots in a particular election, often expressed as a percentage of the total registered voters.

Voting Rights Act (VRA): An act of Congress passed in 1965 to abolish discriminatory voting practices—such as poll taxes, literacy tests, unfair voting schemes, gerrymandering, and language requirements—that restricted the participation of African Americans and other U.S. citizens of color.

War on Poverty: An initiative of the Lyndon Johnson administration that created job training and housing assistance programs in an effort to eliminate poverty.

■ BIBLIOGRAPHY

Acuña, Rodolfo. 1981. *Occupied America: A history of Chicanos*. New York: Harper and Row, 1981.

Affigne, Tony. 2000. Latino politics in the United States: An introduction. *PS: Political Science and Politics* 33(3). Available online at http://www.apsanet.org/PS/sept00/toc.cfm.

Anaya, Rudolfo. 2000. *Elegy on the death of César Chávez*. El Paso, TX: Cinco Puntos Press.

Barrera, Mario. 1979. *Race and class in the Southwest: A theory of racial inequality*. Notre Dame: University of Notre Dame Press.

Bedolla, Lisa Garcia. 2000. They and we: Identity, gender, and politics among Latino youth in Los Angeles. *Social Science Quarterly* 81(1): 106–23.

Blea, Irene I. 1992. *La Chicana and the intersection of race, class, and gender*. New York: Praeger.

Briggs, Vernon M., and Stephen Moore. 1994. *Still an open door? U.S. immigration policy and the American economy*. Washington, DC: American University Press.

Cadena, Gilbert, and Lara Medina. 2004. Liberation theology and social change: Chicanas and Chicanos in the church. In *Chicanas and Chicanos in contemporary society,* ed. Roberto M. De Anda. 2nd ed. Lanham, MD: Rowman and Littlefield.

Calavita, Kitty. 1992. *Inside the state: The bracero program, immigration, and the I.N.S.* New York: Routledge.

Castillo, Pedro G., and Albert Camarillo, eds. 1973. *Furia y muerte: los bandidos Chicanos*. Los Angeles: Aztlán Publications.

CAWP. Elección Latina. www.rci.rutgers.edu/~cawp/Eleccion/home.htm.

———. Facts and findings. www.rci.rutgers.edu/~cawp.

Chávez Candelaria, Cordelia, Peter J. García, and Arturo J. Aldama, eds. 2004. *Encyclopedia of Latino popular culture in the United States*. Westport, CT: Greenwood Press.

Cornelius, Wayne A. 1998. The structural embeddedness of demand for Mexican immigrant labor: New evidence from California. In *Crossings: Mexican immigration in interdisciplinary perspectives,* ed. Marcelo Suárez-Orozco. Cambridge, MA: David Rockefeller Center for Latin American Studies, Harvard University.

Darder, Antonia, and Rodolfo D. Torres. 1998. *The Latino studies reader: Culture, economy, and society*. Malden, MA: Blackwell.

de la Garza, Rodolfo O., Louis DeSipio, F. Chris García, John A. García, and Angelo Falcon. 1992. *Latino voices: Mexican, Puerto Rican, and Cuban perspectives on American politics*. Boulder, CO: Westview Press.

de la Garza, Rodolfo O., Angelo Falcon, F. Chris García, and John A. García. 1998. Latino national political survey, 1989–1990. Ann Arbor: Inter-University

Consortium for Political and Social Research, University of Michigan. Available online at http://webapp.icpsr.umich.edu/cocoon/ICPSR-STUDY/06841.xml.

de la Garza, Rodolfo O., and Louis DeSipio. 1997. Save the baby, change the bath-water, and scrub the tub: Latino electoral participation after twenty years of Voting Rights Act coverage. In *Pursuing power: Latinos and the political system*, ed. F. Chris García. Notre Dame, IN: University of Notre Dame Press.

de la Torre, Adela, and Antonio Estrada. 2001. *Mexican Americans and health: ¡Sana! ¡Sana!* Tucson: University of Arizona Press.

DeSipio, Louis. 1996. *Counting on the Latino vote: Latinos as a new electorate*. Char-lottesville: University of Virginia Press.

DeSipio, Louis, and Rodolfo de la Garza. 1998. *Making Americans, remaking America: Immigration and immigrant policy*. Boulder, CO: Westview Press.

Escobar, Edward. 1999. *Race, police, and the making of a political identity: Mexican Americans and the Los Angeles Police Department, 1900–1945*, Berkeley: University of California Press.

Fraga, Luis Ricardo, Kenneth J. Meier, and Robert E. England. 1986. Hispanic Amer-icans and educational policy: Limits to equal access. *Journal of Politics* 48: 850–76.

García, Alma. 2000. The development of Chicana feminism discourse. In *Unequal sisters: A multicultural reader in U.S. women's history*, ed. Vicki L. Ruíz and Ellen Carol DuBois, 531–45. 3rd ed. New York: Routledge.

García, F. Chris. 1974. *La causa política: A Chicano politics reader*. Notre Dame, IN: University of Notre Dame Press.

——. 1997. *Pursuing power: Latinos and the political system*. Notre Dame, IN: Univer-sity of Notre Dame Press.

García, Ignacio M. 1989. *United we win: The rise and fall of La Raza Unida party*. Tucson: Mexican American Studies Research Center, University of Arizona.

García, John A. 2003. *Latino politics in America: Community, culture, and interests*. Oxford: Rowman and Littlefield.

García, John A., and Rodolfo de la Garza. 1985. Mobilizing the Mexican immigrant: The role of Mexican American organizations. *Western Political Quarterly* 38: 551–64.

Gómez-Quiñones, Juan. 1990. *Chicano politics: Reality and promise, 1940–1990*. Albu-querque: University of New Mexico Press.

——. 1994. *Roots of Chicano politics, 1600–1940*. Albuquerque: University of New Mexico Press.

Gordon, Linda. 1999. *The great Arizona orphan abduction*. Cambridge, MA: Harvard University Press.

Grebler, Leo, Joan W. Moore, Ralph C. Guzman, and Jeffrey Lionel Berlant. 1970. *The Mexican American people: The nation's second largest minority*. New York: Free Press.

Grofman, Bernard. 1992. *Minority representation and the quest for voting equality*. Cambridge, MA: Cambridge University Press.

Grofman, Bernard, and Chandler Davidson, eds. 1992. *Controversies in minority voting: The Voting Rights Act in perspective*. Washington, DC: Brookings Institution.

Gutiérrez, David G. 1995. *Walls and mirrors: Mexican Americans, Mexican immigrants, and the politics of ethnicity*. Berkeley: University of California Press.

Hardy-Fanta, Carol. 1993. *Latina politics, Latino politics: Gender, culture, and political participation in Boston*. Philadelphia: Temple University Press.

Hero, Rodney E. 1992. *Latinos and the U.S. political system: Two-tiered pluralism*. Philadelphia: Temple University Press.

Hero, Rodney, and Caroline Tolbert. 1997. Latinos and substantive representation in the U.S. House of Representatives: Direct, indirect, or nonexistent? In *Pursuing power: Latinos and the political system,* ed. F. Chris García. Notre Dame, IN: University of Notre Dame Press.

Hispanics seek power with PLAN. 1995. *Boston Globe.* May 14.

Kanellos, Nicolás, with Cristelia Pérez. 1995. *Chronology of Hispanic-American history: From pre-Columbian times to the present.* New York: Gale Research.

Katz, Friedrich. 1998. *The life and times of Pancho Villa.* Stanford, CA: Stanford University Press.

Keller, Gary D. 1994. *Zapata lives.* Colorado Springs, CO: Maize Press.

Kuttner, Robert. 2001. Latinos help revive labor movement. *San Diego Union-Tribune,* May 6, p G3.

Library of Congress. Hispanic Americans in Congress, 1822–1995. www.loc.gov/rr/hispanic/congress.

Lipsky, Michael. 1980. *Street-level bureaucracy: Dilemmas of the individual in public services*. New York: Russell Sage Foundation.

LULAC. About LULAC. www.lulac.org/About.html.

LWV. Women see responsive role of government. www.lwv.org/elibrary/pub/ladieshj.htm.

Magaña, Lisa. 1999. The implementation of public policies in Latino Los Angeles. *Latino Studies Journal* 10(3): 53–66.

———. 2003. *Straddling the border: Immigration policy and the INS.* Austin: University of Texas Press.

Magaña, Lisa, and Robert Short. 2002. The social construction of Mexican and Cuban immigrants by politicians. *Review of Policy Research* 49(4): 78–94.

Marín, Gerardo, and Barbara VanOss Marín. 1991. *Research with Hispanic populations.* Applied Social Research Methods series no. 23. Newbury Park, CA: Sage Publications.

Marquez, Benjamin. 1985. *Power and politics in a Chicano barrio: A study of mobilization efforts and community power in El Paso.* Lanham, MA: University Press of America.

———. 2003. *Constructing identities in Mexican American oolitical organizations: Choosing issues, taking sides.* Austin: University of Texas Press.

Martínez, Oscar J., ed. 1996. *U.S.–Mexico borderlands: Historical and contemporary perspectives*. Wilmington, DE: Scholarly Resources.

Martínez-Ebers, Valerie, Luis Fraga, Linda Lopez, and Arturo Vega. 2000. Latino interests in education, health, and criminal justice policy. *PS: Political Science and Politics* 33(3). Available online at http://www.apsanet.org/PS/sept00/toc.cfm.

Menjívar, Cecilia. 2000. *Fragmented ties: Salvadoran immigrant networks in America*. Berkeley: University of California Press.

Menjívar, Cecilia, and Lisa Magaña. 2002. Immigration to Arizona: Diversity and change. In *Arizona Hispanics: The evolution of influence,* ed. Louis Olivas. Proceedings of the 81st Arizona Town Hall. Tempe: Arizona State University.

Mirandé, Alfredo, and Evangelina Enríquez. 1979. *La Chicana: The Mexican American woman*. Chicago: University of Chicago Press.

Montejano, David, ed. 1999. *Chicano politics and society in the late twentieth century*. Austin: University of Texas Press.

Montoya, Lisa J., Carol Hardy-Fanta, and Sonia García. 2000. Latina politics: Gender, participation, and leadership. *PS: Political Science and Politics* 33(3). Available online at http://www.apsanet.org/PS/sept00/toc.cfm.

Moore, Joan W., and Henry Pachon. 1985. *Hispanics in the United States*. Englewood Cliffs, NJ: Prentice Hall.

Morales, Rebecca, and Frank Bonilla. 1993. *Latinos in a changing U.S. economy: Comparative perspectives on growing inequality*. Newbury Park, CA: Sage Publications.

NALEO. 1989. *National Latino Immigrant Survey*. Washington, DC: NALEO.

———. 2003. *National directory of Latino elected officials*. Washington, DC: NALEO.

NALEO Educational Fund. Home page. www.naleo.org.

Naples, Nancy A. 1998. *Grassroots warriors: Activist mothering, community work, and the war on poverty*. New York: Routledge.

Niemann, Yolanda Flores, ed. 2002. *Chicana leadership: The frontiers reader*. Lincoln: University of Nebraska Press.

Nyhan, David. 1995. If it plays in California, will it play in the Granite State? *Boston Globe,* September 1, p. 23.

Oboler, Suzanne. 1995. *Ethnic labels, Latino lives: Identity and the politics of (re)presentation in the United States*. Minneapolis: University of Minnesota Press.

Olivas, Louis. 2002. *Arizona Hispanics: The evolution of influence*. 81st Arizona Town Hall. Tempe: Arizona State University.

Pachon, Harry. 1983. Hispanic underrepresentation in the federal bureaucracy: The missing link in the policy process for Latinos and the political system. In *The state of Chicano research on family, labor, and migration: Proceedings of the first Stanford symposium on Chicano research and public policy,* ed. Armando Valdez, Albert Camarillo, and Tomás Almaguer. Stanford: Stanford Center for Chicano Research.

Pardo, Mary S. 1997. Mexican American grassroots community activists: Mothers of

East Los Angeles. In *Pursuing power: Latinos and the political system,* ed. F. Chris García. Notre Dame, IN: University of Notre Dame Press.

———. 1998. *Mexican American women activists: Identity and resistance in two Los Angeles communities.* Philadelphia: Temple University Press.

Pastor, Manuel. 1993. Latinos and the Los Angeles uprising: The economic context. Report. Los Angeles, CA: Tomás Rivera Policy Institute.

Peterson, Paul E. 1981. *City limits.* Chicago: University of Chicago Press.

Polinard, J. L. 1994. *Electoral structure and urban policy: The impact on Mexican American communities.* Armonk, NY: M. E. Sharpe.

Prindeville, Diane-Michele, and John G. Bretting. 1998. Indigenous women activists and political participation: The case of environmental justice. *Women and Politics* 19(1): 39–58.

Pulido, Laura. 1996. *Environmentalism and economic justice: Two Chicano struggles in the Southwest.* Tucson: University of Arizona Press.

Riddell, Adaljiza Sosa. 1974. Chicanas en el movimento. *Aztlan* 5:155–65.

Rodríguez, David. 2002. *Latino national political coalitions: Struggles and challenges.* New York: Routledge.

Rodriguez, Roberto. 1996. The origins and history of the Chicano Movement. JSRI Research and Publications Occasional Paper No. 7. East Lansing, MI: Julian Samora Research Institute, Michigan State University. Available online at http://www.jsri.msu.edu/RandS/research/ops/oco7abs.html.

Roeser, Thomas. 2003. Latino poll could be GOP's gain. *Chicago Sun-Times,* February 1, p. 14.

Ruíz, Vicki L. 1998. *From out of the shadows: Mexican women in twentieth-century America.* New York: Oxford University Press.

Ruíz, Vicki L., and Ellen Carol DuBois. 2000. *Unequal sisters: A multicultural reader in U.S. women's history.* 3rd ed. New York: Routledge.

Saito, Leland T. 1998. *Race and politics: Asian Americans, Latinos, and Whites in a Los Angeles suburb.* Urbana: University of Illinois Press.

Saldívar-Hull, Sonia. 2000. *Feminism on the border: Chicana gender politics and literature.* Berkeley: University of California Press.

Sánchez, George J. 1993. *Becoming Mexican American: Ethnicity, culture, and identity in Chicano Los Angeles, 1900–1945.* New York: Oxford University Press.

Sánchez, Leonel. 2003. Poverty expands its reach: "Pockets" of poor in San Diego County more than double in number over decade. *San Diego Union-Tribune,* May 18.

Sierra, Christine Marie, and Adaljisa Sosa-Riddell. 1994. Chicanas as political actors: Rare literature, complex practice. *National Political Science Review* 4: 297–317.

Suárez-Orozco Marcelo M., ed. 1998. *Crossings: Mexican immigration in interdisciplinary perspectives.* Cambridge, MA: David Rockefeller Center for Latin American Studies, Harvard University.

Suro, Roberto. 1998. *Strangers among us: How Latino immigration is transforming America*. New York: Alfred A. Knopf.

Synovate Research. 2002. *2002 U.S. Hispanic market report*. Chicago: Synovate Research.

———. 2004. *2004 U.S. Hispanic market report*. Chicago: Synovate Research.

Takaki, Ronald, ed. 1994. *From different shores: Perspectives on race and ethnicity in America*. New York: Oxford University Press.

Takash, P. 1993. Breaking barriers to representation: Chicana/Latina elected officials in California. *Urban Anthropology* 22: 325–60.

Texas State Historical Association. The handbook of Texas online. www.tsha.utexas.edu/handbook/online/articles/view/LL/we11.html.

Therrien, Melissa, and Roberto R. Ramirez. 2000. *The Hispanic population in the United States: March 2000*. Current Population Reports, P20-535. Washington, D.C.: U.S. Census Bureau.

Torres, Rodolfo D., and George Katsiaficas. 1999. *Latino social movements, historical and theoretical perspectives: A new political science reader*. New York: Routledge.

United Farm Workers of America. History, Dolores Huerta biography. www.ufw.org.

United States House of Representatives. Representative web sites. www.house.gov/pastor, www.house.gov/roybal-allard, www.lindasanchez.house.gov, and www.lorettasanchez.house.gov.

U.S. Census Bureau. 2000a. Current population reports: Voting and registration in the election of 2000. Available online at http://www.census.gov/prod/2002pubs/p20-542.pdf.

U.S. Census Bureau. 2000b. Current population survey, March 2000. Available online at www.bls.census.gov/cps/cpsmain.htm.

———. 2004. U.S. Interim projections by age, sex, race, and Hispanic origin. Available online at www.census.gov/ipc/www/usinterimproj.

Verba, Sidney, Kay Lehman Schlozman, and Henry E. Brady. 1995. *Voice and equality: Civic voluntarism in American politics*. Cambridge, MA: Harvard University Press.

Villarreal, Roberto, E., Norma G. Hernandez, and Howard D. Neighbor, eds. 1988. *Latino empowerment: Progress, problems, and prospects*. New York: Greenwood Press.

Wolfinger, Raymond E. 1965. The development and persistence of ethnic voting. *American Political Science Review* 59: 896–908.

Yoachum, Susan. 1994. Small minority voter turnout a product of apathy and anger. *San Francisco Chronicle*. September 22.

■ INDEX

ABOUT THE AUTHOR

LISA MAGAÑA is an associate professor in the Department of Chicana/o Studies at Arizona State University. She received her doctorate from the Center for Politics and Economics at Claremont Graduate University. She has published in the area of immigration and Latino public policy issues in such periodicals as the *Harvard Hispanic Policy Journal,* the *Journal of Policy Studies,* and the *Journal of Social Psychology.* She is the author of *Straddling the Border* (University of Texas Press, 2003) and the editor of *Mexican Americans: Are They an Ambivalent Minority?* (Tomás Rivera Center, 1994).

Dr. Magaña has been a research associate at the Tomás Rivera Policy Institute and visiting lecturer and assistant professor at Pitzer College, the University of California at Los Angeles, and Williams College.

Mexican Americans and the Politics of Diversity is a volume in the series The Mexican American Experience, a cluster of modular texts designed to provide greater flexibility in undergraduate education. Each book deals with a single topic concerning the Mexican American population. Instructors can create a semester-length course from any combination of volumes, or may choose to use one or two volumes to complement other texts.

Additional volumes deal with the following subjects:

Mexican Americans and Health
Adela de la Torre and Antonio Estrada

Chicano Popular Culture
Charles M. Tatum

Mexican Americans and the U.S. Economy
Arturo González

Mexican Americans and the Law
Reynaldo Anaya Valencia, Sonia R. García, Henry Flores, and José Roberto Juárez Jr.

Chicana/o Identity in a Changing U.S. Society
Aída Hurtado and Patricia Gurin

Mexican Americans and the Environment
Devon G. Peña

For more information, please visit
www.uapress.arizona.edu/textbooks/latino.htm